Lessons *in* Lasagna

Ingredient Counseling *from a* Mafia Daughter

By

Luann Puglisi Kenmore

authorHOUSE®

AuthorHouse™
1663 Liberty Drive
Bloomington, IN 47403
www.authorhouse.com
Phone: 1 (800) 839-8640

This book is a work of non-fiction. Names of people and places have been changed to protect their privacy.

Published by AuthorHouse   03/20/2015

ISBN: 978-1-4184-8539-9 (sc)
ISBN: 978-1-4184-8538-2 (hc)

Library of Congress Control Number: 2004096142

Print information available on the last page.

Any people depicted in stock imagery provided by Thinkstock are models, and such images are being used for illustrative purposes only. Certain stock imagery © Thinkstock.

This book is printed on acid-free paper.

This book is dedicated to my husband and my children for loving me more than I ever thought possible and for encouraging me to move forward when I thought I couldn't. Also, thanks Mom - for having and raising me. And to my Nani — who's soft hands I miss every day.

AUTHORS NOTE

I have mentioned in this book; continuously, new information surfaces pertaining to my dad; his vanishing, his connections to the Mafia, their role in his present state of being or evacuation of. Excitingly, two recent and by far the most intriguing leads contributing to the unraveling of this mystery will be posted on my web site: www.Lessons in Lasagna.com. As these discoveries are imperative; hinging on corroboration of the truths; each moment leading to his vanishing, each unearthing of the mystery; further enabling me to inscribe the companion to this book. Twenty five years of unknowing, my fears have subsided; at least most of the people who could cause myself or my family harm, are likely dead, or too old to care. No matter; I will persevere, it is in my blood; his blood, to seek. I will it, for myself, and others like me; our loved ones vanish from our arms, left pregnant with unanswered questions; and vacancies in our hearts.

INCEPTION

After my father disappeared—and my funding—I returned to waiting tables and closet writing. I moved to California, got married, and had two amazing kids, and through the process of filling these new roles, I got lost. A notable amount of time passed before I was encouraged to put aside my fear of rejection and expose myself publicly—to tell a story that would put some loose ends to rest.

While figuring out how to put these words together with a binding, I was asked whom I was writing this for; I took that as a sort of insinuation that perhaps no one would want to read this book. After some thought and inner examination, I knew the answer to the question; I decided it was me. I am the giver and the receiver; I wrote for myself. It's my truth, simply put. It became my opportunity to assemble the chaos of my past into a viable means of self-expression—a slather of peace in my room of tortures.

I wrote it as though I were building a house, all the while planning its housewarming party. I had some difficulty staying focused. Building the foundation before putting up curtains, so many memories, emotions, and incidents I'd buried resurfaced. I found myself going off on tangents, so, in the end, I'd let myself go, then reeled myself in by re-editing over and over.

In a sense, it was like preparing a recipe, adding and subtracting ingredients until the flavor is satisfying. As a writer, I have potential. But I am hard on myself. Foolishly, I feared what others thought;

I trusted their judgment more than my own. It seemed everyone wanted to edit my thoughts, perhaps because they hadn't spoken their own. In this process of exposing myself, I found I could be easily crushed; I concealed it well. When you consider yourself to be an outsider, whether by virtue or proxy, you define yourself by others—at least I did.

It's a precarious, unbalanced way to exist. I found myself sighing a lot, and, eventually, I couldn't breathe. I carried a paper bag around with me for a long time feeling hypersensitive to criticism from people whose outlook shouldn't matter to me. I proceeded fighting my roundness into their square fittings; it never felt right. I attempted several means to overcome self-deprecation; most were unsuccessful. Then I decided, "Screw it—what's the worst thing that could happen?" So people walked away saying, "What was she thinking?"

I didn't care; the reality is I am already a success in my life. I have a great family, which I prize caring for, a landscape of friends and acquaintances, and a home that is my haven. I laugh, cook, garden, read, socialize, and play with my husband, kids, and dogs. We are healthy, have a strong faith, and are complete in the knowledge of our comforts. I am kind because it feels good, and, slowly, I am learning to receive. Anything else is like fries with a garden burger—the burger is good on its own; the fries are merely enhancers.

With these revelations in place, I focused on where my comforts lie. Two activities I felt sufficiently confident doing are writing and cooking. I express myself through both; together, they have become my scaffolding. I don't pretend to be a genius at either. I am a woman grappling with healing, and embracing and valuing mortality; I get that it is temporary.

I have a willingness to keep going, which is why I wrote this. I meet a lot of people haunted and ashamed by their struggles. I have been stalked by shame myself—and still am, though less and less. It felt good to open the attic and release its haunting inhabitants.

I invite you to leave any ghosts, fears, or shame in the blank pages I have provided at the end of this book. I have and will continue to expose them all—perhaps through fiction as to protect my personal life, but I will do it. I have a feeling that if I am done with this process, I may not need to be here anymore. So I embrace all of the old and new inhabitants. There are definitely ones who are stubborn and need to go, so I continue.

GROUNDWORK

I grew up in the Hamptons in the '60s and '70s. It was great—and not.

My unusual family moved to Westhampton Beach when I was going into the second grade. On the first day of school, Sheila, a heavy, black girl in front of me, peed in her seat because the teacher was old and prejudiced and thought she should hold it. Kids are robbed early of their rights and their dignity; I was no exception. Because of my heritage—we were Italians in the restaurant/bar business, which was a hard act in a small, Waspy town—I stood in the corner a great deal of the time, mainly because I was shy when called on and deemed early on to be below average. It didn't help that I became a "social butterfly" or "chatty" to overcome my feelings of inadequacy.

Italians were not welcome at the country clubs, so we knew a little about prejudice. I do not claim to assemble myself in the same line as those severely discriminated against; I had empathy for them, though. In our family, we had our own way of overcoming this kind of hurdle: We all had the "charisma" gene and managed, through our own use of it, to make a place for ourselves in that community of old money and related locals. Humor and comedy also graced our tool box, so that was helpful.

The community we immigrated into was practically one family—almost everyone was related through some distant blood tie. Though it was never confirmed within our family, it was rumored that my father was affiliated with the Mafia, a fact revealed in 1980 when he was arrested for embezzlement and his connections with a Mafia crime family, the Colombos. Imagine my surprise.

Then, a few years ago, a friend found Daddy's name in the Mafia Encyclopedia, a sort of Who's Who in the mob. That revelation was shocking, though I admit in some small, perverse way, satisfying. We are born into situations beyond our control until we are of age to modify our circumstances—becoming adults, making other decisions to alter future events, and the like. Even then, there are only so many ways people can amend their family recipes. We learn a way to do something because we see it done over and over. Traits of our ancestors, an underlying fear of becoming Mom or Dad, and negative or positive inheritance are inevitable.

Much of my youth was a series of gossip and innuendos. I was a tenderhearted, petite girl who pretended to laugh when cruelty came my way. Kids are brutal; grownups are worse. Those rumors carried weight. I felt it; I consumed shame. I felt obliged to be so good, so accommodating, so entertaining that I could take the pressure off the family. I tried to get us off the blacklist, and never let on I was feeling this way; I just didn't know I was doing it.

Our daddy disappeared forever on Valentine's Day in 1980. Another adjustment. I had a reporter spit glass in my face in Magic's Pub when he found out I was Victor Puglisi's daughter. He had so much rage and hate for my family, yet he had never met one of us—

including my father. His facts were hearsay, as were many that were reported. Yet in a closed mind, that is just as valid. The media had him in Reno murdering the son of one of his "enemies," when I was with him in Florida during that time.

Locals pointed and whispered; some spoke outwardly against him and us. My telephones were tapped, and I was visited by agencies of the government and Mafia I didn't know existed. My friends were scared, and I was fired from my job because of the many visitors who interrupted my work and filled my boss with fear. Most of the visitors wore visible guns to make themselves appear intimidating; it worked with everyone but me. I became defiant and rebellious; it pissed me off.

My friends and I were followed by guys who looked like the cast of the old television show *Dragnet*. Eventually, we were run off the road during a surfing contest in Montauk Point on our way to a square dance. Mysteriously, the driver of the other vehicle disappeared, although he was booked for drunken driving at the scene.

I began to feel threatened as the intent to harm me became very real. I lost all of my teeth from that car accident, though it took the painful part of twenty years for them all to come out. (I am still dealing with the aftereffects, physically and financially.) I learned not to sit on the hump in a car, to always wear a seat belt, and to drive whenever possible. From February 'til November, I was followed and harassed until, eventually, my friends were scared into pointing out my residence. What's a girl to do?

I've been ashamed to tell my story because I'm not proud of a lot of it. I hate being judged. I know I was a victim, but I felt guilty because he was my father; I was tainted and imperfect.

If nothing else, I have learned in the last forty-five years that it doesn't matter—we are judged anyway, often by ourselves. I was a casualty of many crimes, even at four, when a series of molestations were inflicted on me. I felt in some way responsible.

That's messed up, and it's common. I hope after reading my story, others will see the truth: It's ludicrous to blame yourself for crimes committed against you or for attachments to criminals you are related to. It is a self-inflicted crime, however, to hold on to that old, sick thinking when you could focus on happiness.

I was wary launching this book; I didn't want to hurt anyone, get anybody in trouble, or shame my family. But I could not live with all this stuff inside me. I took great pains to present people in a positive light. However, you cannot change history by pretending it didn't happen or by not talking about it.

This is not just my history; every person mentioned in this book is part of my history. Every person you encounter becomes a part of your days gone by. Being connected to dangerous people burdens you—even if your family is famous, your life is distorted. It's life though; you must embrace it all, fight for your honor, stand up for your beliefs, trust your intuition, and, most importantly, live!

After my family was exposed, I wanted to take some control. I needed to have some privacy again—some normalcy. I felt harassed by these men hunting for my father, hungry for imagined information I must be privy to. I was tired of being stared at, talked about, and threatened. I so desperately wanted to be held and comforted; people were used to me being strong, I suppose, and no one knew me well enough to say, "Hey, you need help."

In an effort to exonerate myself from any affiliation with the situation my father left me in, and to stop the invasion of my privacy, I met with Arthur Findlay, the Godfather of the IRS. He looked like a mobster. He was tall and imposing, gray-haired in a dark, pinstriped suit, wearing a tie clip with a twinkling diamond in its rough, gold design. His skin was not smooth; it was wrinkled where he furrowed from stress and pocked in areas from adolescent acne or chicken pox. His demeanor was decidedly one of a man trying to look intimidating; his deep-set voice boomed from his long, unsmiling face. He had dark eyes deeply set under bushy, graying eyebrows. I considered his the safest organization to encounter, since everyone else seemed worse.

He came to my home, escorted by two goons. They could have worked for my father; perhaps they did. It was a hot, August day. Minutes earlier, I had returned from the beach. I was preparing to shower when they knocked. The goons were overly anxious to enter, and one guy shoved his foot in the doorway, forcing the door open. Still wearing my string bikini from Judith Powers, I endured their interrogation. After several variations of the same questions in an effort to catch me in a lie, I inquired of Mr. Findlay, "Do you have children of your own?"

"Yes, I do," my interrogator answered.

I pried, "How old are they?"

"About your age," his lips twitched, and I felt that he fought a smile when he responded.

I stared at this man, his gray hair beading with perspiration in the humid stillness of our enclosed patio.

"Mr. Findlay, do you discuss your work with your children?" I asked.

"Certainly not!" he countered indignantly.

"Then what would make you think my father would discuss his business with *me*? I barely saw my father. He loved me and I, him, and now he's gone," I said. "That's all I know."

He looked long and hard into my eyes before standing and extending his sweaty hand. "Thank you for your time, Miss Puglisi," he said. "I'm sorry for your loss."

I believed him.

Though my childhood was laced with the horrors of molestation and chaos, it happened, and it wasn't my fault. How I dealt with it was. I was on my own and I made many wrong decisions, but I grew from every one of them.

If my father hadn't disappeared and I hadn't been in a car accident, I probably would not have flown back to California with burgundy and pink stripes in my hair, a bicycle, and a duffle bag with my collection of *Cosmopolitan* magazines to be with my mother. I would not have gotten a job through my mom's friend, met my mother-in-law, and married her son. I would not be living in suburbia, which is providing my kids with the freedom to explore, build forts, ride bikes, have an atmosphere with kids to play with, and grow up with what I enjoyed as a child, surrounded by other kids. And I hope for a better chance at normalcy, whatever that turns out to be for them.

I intended for this record of events to establish an example to my kids and whoever reads this book that stuff happens, often beyond our control. It took a long time to make this choice; by sharing my stories, I chose to compost my shit and grow flowers, using food and words as my vehicle. I hope that after reading this, you will find your vehicle and begin your healing process—and find humor in it on the way.

ABOUT THE AUTHOR

Having been asked some poignant questions about how she ended up a suburban stay-at-home mother and wife; retracing her history and her path: Luann P. Kenmore concluded her scaffolding has been a culmination of cooking and writing; one a life line, the other a life source. Through personal revelations of her father's connection to the Mafia, his disappearance after 23 years with no closure; she has compiled painful, funny, even awful events in detailed vignettes; served with recipes she now relinquishes. Reconstructing some haunting realizations of a life she observed with outward sight; she now uses her memories returned to her through this journey of food and words to gain inward sight. Her hunger to be independent of emotional baggage has driven her to intertwine two skills to keep her footing. A zesty, funny and emotional journey concluding the ends and beginnings of triumphant acceptance of unnatural circumstance and choices creates a venue for her menu. Life is never a singular journey, it is accompanied by those who stay forever and some who pass through like a breath; enriched by these characters crowding her stage, even the ones there to hurt her directed her in some way, forward.

TABLE OF CONTENTS

LAYER 1

Lessons in Lasagna

"Sometimes being too nice can kill ya."

In the beginning, when he first disappeared, I expected to hear from him. He had an uncanny gift for finding me—like the time I was wooed to Florida with my boss from the East Motel, Stan.

I was eighteen and seriously lost. In an effort to earn some money and find a place to live, I hooked up with Claire, a young woman I barely knew from work. Stan, her husband, was a fast-talking Brooklyn Jew; I wish I'd known better than to trust him. He paid a lot of attention to me, and after awhile, Claire began treating me like an employee in her home. She expected me to clean; she even requested I clean her bathroom, which I did.

I can understand her feelings. Stan was flirty, and she had reason not to trust him. But she did invite me to move in with them, therefore setting me up in a way, and I was vulnerable and trusting. She knew her husband's history and could have saved us both a lot of heartache if she had protected me from him. She was older; I trusted and needed a friend.

They were moving from the hotel into their home, a lovely A-frame set back on a big lot in a woodsy area in one of lush Hampton towns. They needed extra help between the move and the hotel, and I was happy to be needed—being needed is a definite flaw in my character. I had a crush on one of Claire's cousins, but he was not interested in me. I felt rejected, and that coupled with my low self-esteem, no sense of me, and little faith in my own instincts left me vulnerable. My ability to tap into me was hidden.

Claire was a Princess; I was a local. She got to be a camp counselor; I grew up serving people like her in my parents' restaurants and cleaning their big condos on the beach. No complaints. Some of the people I worked for were demanding and obnoxious, but they weren't cheap, and they certainly were not out to belittle me. Some of my favorite clients were the Solomons. They were a wonderful, generous couple. For my thirteenth birthday, they gave me two tickets to see Elvis Presley. It was the most amazing concert I have ever seen! We were in the seventh row, behind the wheelchairs. When Elvis threw his white silk scarf into the crowd, I had it in my hands. But the lady in front of us had it, too, and since we were standing on our chairs and she was in a wheelchair, we let her have it. I never saw anyone cry so hard; it was as though Elvis was her lover. I was glad we could give that gift to her.

The Solomons respected and cared about our lives. Because of Mrs. Solomon, I am a fanatic about water spots on the chrome in the bathroom and kitchen. She was particular, and so am I. I learned a great deal about how to relate to my own employees with respect and dignity through her treatment of me.

The difference between the Solomons and Claire and Stan is that I never felt degraded by the Solomons. They were classy and kind. I enjoyed being around them, and their faith and rituals interested me. They were genuine.

Stan and Claire acted like they were above me. I was insecure, and I let myself feel like I was a lesser person. I was unsure of myself and in my ignorance; I was seduced into their life of parties and immorality. I didn't know any enlightened women then, so I mistook Claire for one. She was young, married to a seemingly successful man, and she had security. I thought she had it all.

After my father left us, my mother moved men in and out of our lives. It seemed normal to be compromised. No offense to her—loneliness is a dangerous roommate. On the other hand, it made me fiercely independent, suspicious, and vulnerable. I also felt that the defining happiness of my life would be found in a man. I looked for myself in many people; I was never in there, though.

When there were vacancies at the hotel, I took a room, glad to be out of their house, happy to be alone. In May or early June, I had taken a long, hot shower and crawled into bed early. Stan snuck in with the master key. I woke feeling like I was being watched—and I was. I felt flattered and scared. He said he was leaving for a business trip and needed me to go with him as his assistant, and that he would take me to my father in Hollywood, Florida.

I jumped at the opportunity to be away from there and to be with my father. I needed to be with him; I needed to feel connected. Stan thought it best that Claire didn't know. She'd get the wrong idea, he said, and she'd have been right. I was so naïve.

I felt misplaced, and angry with my mother. She was living in a one-bedroom apartment nearly forty miles away from where we called home, paid for by her jealous boyfriend who had a psycho wife and son just itching to kill one of us. Mr. Wonderful's wife cornered me in the bathroom of his restaurant when I was seventeen and threatened me. She put her hands around my throat and suggested she would squeeze tighter if I didn't leave right away.. . . .

There was no room or home for me anywhere. It was the first time I didn't have my own bed and things in one room. I felt like a foreigner. This feeling ran deeper than just a physical address, and it took many years to feel at home in my skin.

After my first year at Alfred University, my father bounced my tuition check. I was not a good student, either. I had no future prospects. My father didn't finish high school, so education was

4

not a priority for him. His philosophy was: "I didn't go to school, and look at me." He'd say this while flashing his fully ring-adorned fingers. He was a very confident man; I was humiliated and lonely. I wanted a quick fix, and being with Stan and Claire seemed like just the ticket—a place to stay and work, and they could be very fun.

I went with Stan and didn't tell my mother. I was angry with her; she was engaged in an unhealthy relationship and had no time or room for me. So I stole a book by John Updike that she was reading and her favorite halter top, and I took off in Stan's Thunderbird.

On the way to Florida, we made a few stops to visit some friends of his, and then we went to the Keys: Marathon and Key West. Stan was moody and horrible to me, demanding for me to be with him, and threatening to leave me there if I didn't do what he asked. He drank and smoked pot, which made him moody and tired. He criticized me when I wouldn't do what he wanted me to do, and lied about taking me to my father's.

His birthday occurred during the trip, and I bought him a shirt and a pair of shorts. He didn't like them and said it was stupid of me to spend the money, which it was. I considered calling Daddy, but didn't want to seem helpless. I knew I had made a really bad choice by coming on this spree, and I was deeply ashamed of myself and scared. The last thing I wanted was an "I told you so" from dear Dad.

One begrudgingly muggy night, I was reading in the bathroom because it had a lock on the door. Stan was sleeping off a few rum and Cokes. The phone rang; it was my father. Stan paled through his tropical tan, and handed me the phone.

"Daughter, what are ya thinking sneaking away with this creep? You can't hide from me. Who is this guy anyway? You worried your mother. She says he's married, for God sakes! Go home, now!"

"Well, isn't she one to talk! I don't have a home!" I said, slamming the phone down.

Stan freaked. I was annoyed and secretly relieved, but anxious. I knew something unpleasant was going to happen, and I threw up three times.

On the way home, we stopped in Georgetown, Washington. At first it was exciting. Stan bought me a wooden box with a brass rose on it, and I thought he wasn't mad anymore. But Stan was a sex maniac and wouldn't let me eat unless I gave him satisfaction. He threatened to leave me there; I should have said, "Fine." I was not giving in to his disgusting demands, and I was starving by the time we got to his house.

I called Geraldine, my best friend since the fourth grade. I didn't know if she was home from college, but I had to get out of there. I had borrowed the car to get my stuff from the hotel and was going to stay with Geraldine for a few days.

Her home was my home while I was growing up. Between Geraldine's and the Everetts, I felt some sense of security and normalcy. They had the kind of families I wanted.

I had a bad feeling before I left the hotel, and I knew as I drove away that I should not have left any stuff behind. While I was gone, Claire went through my cosmetics bag and found matches from the hotel she knew Stan had been at.

After I returned and was showering, they demanded that I leave without payment for the month I worked for them. She threw my stuff out of my room, and if Stan hadn't held her back, she would have pulled me right out of the shower. She called me every curse word in the book—and then some.

I never did get the rest of my clothes, and I missed my only pair of jeans. I called my father because I needed a ride from the hotel. He sent Fletcher, whose seven-foot appearance kept everyone at bay, and Fletcher drove me to Geraldine's. I stayed one night there, but they had a full house. Daddy left a ticket for Braniff Airlines at JFK so I could go to Florida until the restaurants got busier, and I knew I could get a job and share a place to live with someone.

When I told Daddy that Stan didn't pay me, he asked for Stan's phone number and proceeded to charge phone calls to Stan's telephone number. When Stan got the bill, he tracked me to my dad's and threatened me—I mean nasty, awful, menacing words. It was said my father paid him a visit to the hotel. Stan called me once more, pissed. He threatened me and warned me to stay out of his sight; I never heard from him again.

Claire trashed my name for years. Sadly, I was accustomed to living with negative publicity: "Your mother's a barmaid and a hooker"; "Your father's in the Mafia and sleeps around"; "My mother saw your father with a blonde last night. Isn't your mother a brunette?"

I was sorry about that unfortunate incident because I sort of liked Claire. I felt terrible guilt. Claire needed a scapegoat to save face; I owed her that, I guess. Her plight was much worse than mine living with a few more rumors. Stan was foul and a philanderer, cheat, and underhanded business dealer. I would have liked to apologize to Claire had I been given the opportunity. I prayed that in her heart, she would know someday.

Claire, if you ever read this, and know that this is you, I really am sorry. I liked you much more than Stan, who I thought was a low-class loser compared to you, even if you did wear that awful blue eye shadow.

Before Dad disappeared, I bounced around like a Gypsy— Florida in the winter; New York in the spring, summer, and fall. I lived with friends in group homes and had no roots or goals. I hooked up with men, hoping they would love me and want to marry me. I wanted my own home and children. By the time 1980 hit, I was becoming a local loser.

On that fateful Valentine's Day, we got a snow storm that equaled my life—a blizzard with zero visibility. It was also the last day I spoke to my father; I would not know security again until I met my husband in 1983. I didn't truly feel secure after I graduated from high school, and my mother started moving around without provisions for me. But at least I knew my father was out there somewhere.

When Daddy left, I had no safety net. The year before, I drove with my mother and two friends to California, but I had a hard time finding a good paying job. I was lonely, and I went home in January. I had some family up the Island, but here, in my hometown, I was truly alone. It was a terrible time for me.

My mother's love, Mr. Wonderful, had a crazy son who enjoyed threatening Mom with bodily harm, and true to his word, he punched her in the chest. He was a bulky "Italian stallion"; she was a petite forty-year-old. Mom wouldn't allow me to tell my father or brother, so I said, "Pack. We're out of here."

We had an awesome cross-country trip. It began with a heartbreaking goodbye between my mom and her lover on a cold morning after an early snow had fallen onto an unyielding earth. We cried for her; we cried for ourselves.

You cannot imagine the trouble four women running away can find. We got lost in a parking lot in Texas, I swear. We drove past what is now known as the Cadillac Ranch, which was later seen on the cover of Bruce Springsteen's album. To behold this sight in the glow of the sunrise of Texas's incredible horizon was bazaar and awesome. The sky was omnipotent, going on forever, colors like a painter's wheel; there are no significant words to do it justice.

Here we were coming off a long night of splurging; we ate real food, had a few drinks, and were entertained by a singer who we thought was Crystal Gale's sister in a lounge in a Holiday Inn. We left Amarillo, (I believe), driving in circles in a maze they called a parking lot, finally seeing an exit and finding the highway.

*BK was afraid to drive on the highway and nervously turned on the windshield wipers instead of the lights, which smeared all the dead bugs we'd collected across the glass and made it impossible to see. We had no water and tried pouring nail polish remover on the glass, which made it worse.

I drove, while everyone slept. For miles, there was nothing more than sterile land, tumbleweeds, and a few tall cacti reaching to the sky for water, it seemed. The sun began seeping through the blackness, lighting up the sky.

To my amazement, there appeared to be at least fifty pink Cadillacs stuck nose-down into the barren earth. I awakened everyone to reassure myself that I was not having hallucinations. Sadly, none of us had film. It was so amazing. No one believed us for years, and we didn't talk about it until we saw the cover of the album by Springsteen. It was only one of the many fun experiences we shared on that trip across the country.

When we got to Arizona, we were bound for the Grand Canyon. We had reservations at a lodge in the Canyon so we could awaken and see it with the sun rising.

The evening before, we ate and drank in the hotel's restaurant, where we met "Swizzle Sticks." He was a local who did mule tours in the canyon. We named him Swizzle Sticks because he had a mustache that was at least six inches straight out from the top of his lip on both sides!

So, in an effort to wake up early, we had the hotel wake us up at 4:30 a.m., which would give us plenty of time to make the twenty-minute ride into the canyon. We were still hung over—having gone to sleep at about 2 a.m.—and the drive seemed interminable, though incredible. The trees were still turning, and it was a magnificent ride.

My mother's impatience lead us to pull over, and there, in a small clearing, arose a chasm that took our breath away. There were rock platforms jutting out over the canyon, and we saw a small group of young people sitting with a bottle of Ripple and passing around a joint. Still in awe, we parked the car and climbed out onto an adjoining dais. Silently, we were absorbing God's work when my mother blurted out, "Hey, where's the faces?" There are few words to describe our mortification. One of the guys on the other platform said, with dripping sarcasm, "Lady, that's Mount Rushmore."

'Nuf said.

Later, we drove through the Painted Desert. We were all thirsty, and my mother, in another act of brilliance, suggested we eat all the salty foods we accumulated on the trip. Her philosophy was that it would make our mouths water, therefore creating more saliva.

So, there you go. It was a trip filled with humor, bonding, and growth between four women of different ages battling similar issues. I thank my mom and give her a lot of credit for her gameness.

That journey, however, was the beginning of a long period of "homelessness" for me. California was filled with beautiful blondes with blue and green eyes, perfect bodies, good jobs, friends, and boyfriends. I couldn't hold a candle. I felt the beginnings of failure set in; I sensed I could offer few skills, save for years in the restaurant business.

I would have liked to finish school. I wanted to be a journalist, but I couldn't afford tuition for San Diego State and living expenses. I was accepted, and that felt good. If I had been a hard-shell crab, I may have found a way; alas, I was a limp soft-shell number, caught up in my own net of self-depreciation. California, though aesthetically perfect, lacked depth and hominess. People in the business had a "cool apathy," and everyone was waiting to become someone else. It was a weird concept, and I never got used to it. It just didn't work for me to try to be someone or something I am not.

One of the girls left before we migrated to Westwood. The other girl and I got jobs in Marina del Rey—she, a bookkeeper; me, a lowly hostess. Mom lied about all kinds of stuff and landed a job in Brentwood. I was more miserable, insecure, and lonely than ever.

Living with three of us in a tiny, unfurnished apartment with one car to share was getting old. I was accustomed to making $60 to $100 per night; at TGI Friday's I barely earned $100 every two weeks. I had a crush on a guy who played a very dirty trick on me, and finally, I let my father send for me.

In 1980, I came back to California after my dad disappeared I was in a car accident in which a guy rammed us into a ditch three times. The police caught him, and, mysteriously, he got away. My mother was fearful for my life. Having lived with my father and his secret dealings, she knew what kind of characters he surrounded himself with. So I boarded a plane and flew back to the West Coast to try it again.

I waded through murky waters for a few more years, then, in 1983, I met my husband. My husband was my first real boyfriend and the only man who really loved me.

Ten years went by, and still no word from Daddy. I tried to investigate his disappearance, to no avail. I had no real clues. People whom I expected to help me, people my father had helped, abandoned me, and some disappeared themselves. Every few years, Daddy's name would come up—someone would ask, or I'd come across articles and I would half-heartedly pick up the search. For a while, some agency would come to my home, asking if I'd had contact with him. An agent came to the hospital after my first child was born; I didn't hear much after that.

I shared my story with a few friends and even pursued a television movie prospect with Ron, a producer I came to know through a girl I acted in a few plays with. It never came to fruition; they wanted a true ending with closure. "Tell me about it," I thought.

My friend wanted me to fudge an ending that would make these people happy. I kept thinking, "What if someday he shows up, or his body is found?" Their motivation felt superficial. I wanted, desperately needed, closure more than they did. Every avenue seemed dead, yet I dreamt about him.

I went to psychics—famous ones who Shirley McClain had gone to and written about. They all said he wasn't dead. I'd dream I'd see him turning a corner, always unable to catch up to him. In some of my dreams, I would come face-to-face with him in public places and at parties. He would look at me like I was crazy, surrounded by women and sometimes girls my age, and he'd say, "What's your problem?"

I'd wake up, crying.

"I've been here the whole time," he would say before he vanished again, his eyes, blue, watery pools.

He always left me with a feeling that he was happier where he was; that he's moved on. I wanted him to become a fading memory in my sentimental heart. I glorified him for a very long time—too long. Pained and anguished by his and my own lost status, I put myself through hell.

Having children became a salve. The more involved in being my children's parent I became, a light went on; I recognized his limited abilities and desire to father me.

I realized that not only had he abandoned us, but he'd put us in very real danger. I disliked him for a long time, and then I began investigating his case again, which has been, in a weird way, cathartic. I bought several books on the Mafia, looking for mention of his name and more clues.

My search continues, though I have little expectation for a permanent sealant against the storms of emotion I can still experience. I have a flicker of hope, and that sustains me, as well as pains me.

I did have an interesting experience a few years ago in Brentwood, California. I was caring for Patti, my friend/ mother-in-law. She was dying of lung cancer. One particularly horrible day, after taking her for her chemotherapy, her vein collapsed, and blood erupted from her withered arm like a geyser. Her face lost every ounce of color. I watched, horrified, as Nurse Mary changed gauze after gauze, holding the area as tightly as she could, while Patti cried about the drop of blood soaking into her new, pink sneakers.

When we got to her apartment, she hit the bathroom a couple of times and missed a couple more. She felt degraded; I felt helpless. I got her settled down, and I took off for a power walk; I was overwrought and my emotions were fried. I found myself on Montana; I had walked two miles, if not more, in twenty-five minutes.

As I stopped for a swig of water, my nose caught the scent of cigar smoke—my father's brand. There was no one there—no one.

I said inside my head, "Daddy, where are you? Are you dead or alive?"

I heard, "It's all the same; I'm with you."

The smell stayed for under a minute, and I lapped it up like a melting ice cream cone in July. Then, I felt a peace fall over me, and my skin rippled with goose bumps. I sighed and realized I was crying. It was a different cry— not so much regret as resolve. I walked back to Patti's enjoying the smells of spring and the laughter of children playing outside longer as the sun held its place in the sky.

When Patti died, I experienced an awareness of relief. I would not have wanted to see my father withered, suffering, or crumpled from the violent shot of a gun. I realized that I had been spared, and through Patti, who shared the same birthday as my father, I was given a kind of resolution that was cleansing and wholesome.

I was born in 1957, an immediate disappointment to my father's lost wager; he wanted another boy. To compensate for my femaleness, he wanted to name me Victoria, though my brother was already named Victor after him. A true Virgo, he was all about himself. Some call it ego; with him it was personality.

My mother named me covertly, while my father celebrated. She enjoyed the independent action, as well as the escape from his family. They disliked her immensely; the feelings were mutual.

They were low-class, demented people. However, in their defense, they probably did the best they knew how to, although knowing two out of three of their sons had problems and ignoring them was not productive. It led their offspring to make problems for themselves—and certainly for others. They thought their babies could do no wrong—even if they beat their wives and cheated on them, and let's not forget abandonment. Well, love really is blind at times, or so it would seem in that family.

I have no love for any of them, except for the their son and his family, who were also victimized. However, they, too, abandoned us in our times of need. So, with out being malicious; or making excuses for them—sad in their own way—I move on.

Living with my father, as my father, became an electric, thrilling, theatrical experience! Electricity is exhilarating, yet disconnected from its power source, darkness descends. That is how I felt when he disappeared. I felt unplugged, and I had no backup generator to rely on; there just weren't enough candles to illuminate my life.

My father lacked "stick-to-it-iveness," abandoning us even while he lived. He would take off and leave us for extended vacations mixed with business, I suppose. He made movies with Mob-related stars—Frank Sinatra, or so they say.

He wished I was a boy, urging me to become a lawyer and stay single, independent, and strong—perhaps anticipating his need for my services someday. He lacked every natural quality a father should possess, but he was mine, and he made me feel special, beautiful, and safe.

He was gone; that's all I knew. His disappearance forever rocked me out of the world I knew. I would never be his baby girl again, and I was not prepared for that wracking; I had never been my mother's, and I never would. She was never as affectionate as he. I did everything wrong from the minute he left. I felt nothing—and everything.

My mother and brother experienced their own forms of detachment, and it was perpetuated by our separation, geographically. My brother was enlisted in the Navy, and my mother was in California. We were stationed on three different coasts, and I was drifting out to sea.

Every bad thing I never thought could happen to me did—in record time. I became the proprietor of my own downfalls; I buried feelings and kept everything hidden. My father taught us to be secretive, to keep ourselves impregnable, and I know why. When you reveal yourself, 5 percent of you—the weak part and your struggles—becomes your label.

I learned the hard way that you can't trust most; people will use your weaknesses to assuage their own issues. Once a criminal, alcoholic, addict, cheater, whatever, that's what people remember. No matter what good you do, you are still labeled, suspect. The minute you make an error, piss someone off or simply behave humanly, that label reappears like a tattoo on your forehead. I understand this human-nature stuff, but it is painful to the labeled. I wore my heart on my sleeve for years, which is why I prefer sleeveless tops.

I wish I had paid more attention to my father's actions. He collected people's weaknesses and deposited them into his account to collect interest. If you crossed him, he withdrew your assets. Loyalty meant security to my father. Then again, I wouldn't really want to be like that—I like who I am. I can forgive people because I know fear and pain cause them to act out. I am, however, much less vulnerable. I let go of those that would hurt me to help themselves. They are numerous and come in every disguise.

Perhaps, this sounds paranoid; so be it. I have learned to protect myself, and I don't care what anyone says about that. Survival is the key to life.

I stopped telling people about my personal life, and began making changes so I could be productive. It hasn't been easy; I still want to know what happened to dear old Dad. I still miss him. I still break down, though it doesn't destroy me the way it did—or not as often. More than the need to answer those questions though, more than the desire to know why, I yearned for a connection that could not be taken from me. My commitment to a spiritual journey kept me moving, while I slowly unpacked my baggage. I still have luggage, just not a full set. Having a loving family with me on my journey has been the difference between failure and success.

When Daddy disappeared, no one—and I mean no one, including my mother—could remember a good thing about him. Only me, and I diluted those small memories to erect him into an icon instead of what he was, which I am still sifting through. He did many favors for people. He was a good son. He loved us—in increments.

He was a sentimental boozer; he would tell us then how much he loved us and how everything he did was for us and our future. I suppose he convinced himself of that unreality. Bottom line though—he left us without warning, provisions, safety, or peace. He chose his life, and he was as true to himself as he could be. And that was a crime against his promise to us, his family.

Looking back, had I been as savvy as my own children, I'd have connected the dots; unexplained events were clearly clues to his posture in life. I wanted to be deceived, I think. I ached to fit. I thrived on the dangerous element of his unknown lifestyle because it made me feel like someone important. It has taken me these twenty-three years to find myself, and I realize now part of the problem was that I was looking for myself in someone else. Living in the shadow of a notorious figure like my father, who, in our small town, in my small life, ferried humongous deficits along with it, carries heavy consequences.

I can't imagine what it is like for kids with political or public figures for parents. There is an unwritten sentiment that if your parents did it, so should or so will you—especially if it carries negative connotations with it. I think my brother has spent much of his life trying to prove he is not my father, when in essence, he is a lot like him—and that is not a bad thing.

I know many women who fear the mere thought of becoming their mothers. I believe the more you fight it, the more it happens. Some transference is inevitable, but no one should have to pay the sins of another. I felt responsible for my father's shortcomings, and I felt tainted by the accusations made against him. I became responsible for those he left behind, except for me. I needed to apologize to his ex-partners, and, more importantly, to have them forgive me.

I felt that writing about him would cancel some of his debt and relieve me of some of my unnecessary obligation to it. Though I realize I am not, could not be, held accountable for his shortcomings, if they could make me a better person, and if I could by proxy do better in the world—my small one and our large one—then so be it.

There are experiences that fell to the recesses of my memory until I began this process. For me, reading and writing trigger those lost episodes of my past. There was so much violence that we ignored—or worse, became accustomed to—which is why I do not watch violent films.

Some of the stuff that happened to us and around us then would be unacceptable to me or to my children. When I was a sophomore in high school and wanted to go on a school trip to Spain, I went to the Riverhead Garden Apartments, an establishment my father owned/occupied, to pick up a check from him. His status/involvement is still unclear to me because he operated from a place of control and ownership in every aspect of his life.

It was a warm spring day. Apple blossoms scented the air surrounding the huge complex, giving it the illusion of being a nice place to live. In a short time, it had been reduced to an unkempt, scary place where gangs of people huddled and stared you down when you entered the structure.

The southeast side was where my father lived; his building was maintained, compared with the rest of the complex. I know my father tried to keep the grounds neat. He was a clean and orderly person, and it disgusted him that the tenants chose to litter and vandalize the grounds faster than his staff could keep it clean. I parked my red Capri and walked the ten feet to the office.

I walked into a chaotic scene: my uncle doubled over, a bloody towel clutched to his abdomen. Fletcher, my father's employee, coddled his hand, the bones of his knuckles exposed with blood squirting from the wound. Police sirens echoed through the compound. I stood in my blue rayon Sizzler dress with the red and white sail boats on it, my face saying all that my words could not.

My father looked up from his position over my uncle. "Go to the apartment," he said. "Umus will give you the money."

Never skipping a beat, moving like a dancer from one man to the next while concealing a bloody knife behind his back, my father was the epitome of composure. I stood long enough for him to usher my uncle into a car and confront the police with his solid explanation of Fletcher's minor injury:

"He was using a skill saw, mending a fence . . . ."

I heard the tale tumble from his thin lips.

Umus was his affectionate name for his live-in girlfriend. She had been on alert, meeting me in the hall with a check, then ushering me into my car and on my way. It happened so fast that it didn't register until I looked down and saw a speck of blood on my white sandals.

That was the last time I wore white sandals, though I never thought about it until now. My brother and I were used to violence or upheaval, I suppose. It didn't register how serious, dangerous, or horrible it was until just now, as I write it out and reread it back.

I have edited these words going on twenty times, including hiring Victoria, a professional editor. I have filed down the violence to protect my family, than inserted more to find a balance. I have been searching for balance my entire life; I'm not sure I have found it still.

Another time, I returned to one of Dad's favorite watering holes in Hampton Bays, the legendary Ed's Bay Pub. I dropped him off after borrowing his white Corvette and ran some errands for him to earn spending money for the weekend. Little did I know that dropping off a suitcase at his house in Flanders would later connect me to his arrest—that and many lunches I attended in which he spoke in hushed tones while I read and ate.

March is not a good month on Long Island, as a rule. The weather is dreary—not quite winter, and not quite spring. It drizzled on and off; the sky was dark with scattered rain clouds, and it was bone-chillingly cold. I drove the back way from Flanders, so I was on side streets, hoping for a glimpse of green gracing the branches of oak trees that lined the windy road. Not even so much as a crocus pushed its yellow face through the unyielding earth. As dark as it was outside, stepping into the cave that was Ed's didn't compare. It smelled of stale cigarettes and my father's cigars—always my father's cigars. We parked in the back, a habit I got from my parents.

My father used to own Ed's, when it was called The Living Room Lounge. My mother ran it; it was a much classier establishment then. The back door allowed a brief amount of light from outside, and a shock of fresh air blew through the stale hallway.

Dad was in the bar with Cricket, my godmother's brother—a Joe Pesci type, though sweeter—who was bloodied from his nose to his lip. He was smiling that sheepish grin, and despite his appearance, I smiled back.

Cricket was a bookie, or so I surmised. I have no real proof of that, though he told me a great story about a place that he and my father ran numbers out of, probably before I was born. They knew they were under surveillance and were supposed to be selling pizzas and God-awful, Early-American-Italian statues. The feds would come in the front door while Rico Balducci and Cricket snuck pizzas from Laperra's in the back door. They didn't get caught because, apparently, my father became a legitimate businessman when he opened the first Hamburger Choo Choo.

Cricket, a character himself, said his wife drove him crazy, so when he was busted about once a year, it gave him a little vacation from her. It was told to us later that he checked himself into jail so he could relax, scratch his balls, and eat Italian food that she didn't cook.

He was a pretty easygoing guy, always singing. When he was high, he'd tell me how pretty I was and how much my father loved me.

"He's proud of you, kiddo. You can't believe how he talks about you and Little Vic," he would say. We heard from his friends how much he bragged about us, but it would have been better to hear it from him.

Inside Ed's, the jukebox played *My Way*, Frank Sinatra crooning my father's mantra, while Daddy sang along. Ed and Cricket laughingly relayed the story of how they had kicked the asses of three punks attempting to blow off an unpaid debt. I could smell blood, and the swelling on Crickets eye made me feel nauseated.

"Daughter, look at your father," he said, holding his arm up to show me his still-hard and bulging muscle. Not bad for an old man."

I smile when I think of his vanity, mine now. He did have a great upper body, and he was fast on his feet like a boxer. I remember few incidences in which he did not go out looking for a brawl; it made him feel young, I think. I wonder if, in his last days, the grip of fear around his throat, all those times he terrified others came back to him.

Daddy was a firm believer in defensive self-defense. In other words, before anyone had a chance to get you, you got to them first. He taught my brother and me how to box. He said I had natural talent, but that was long before women boxed.

I thought of these realities of my father, as I surveyed the empty bar. Broken glass dusted the thin, red carpet now stained with nights of drunken partying, burned and scattered with cigarette butts. Across the pool table, once shiny and kept, two broken cue sticks lay abandoned. I shook my head at the pride the three of them displayed at running the perpetrators from the bar.

Ali smirked at me from behind the bar. She was Eddie's girlfriend, a mousy looking girl with stringy, black hair who never liked me. Too many young girls lost their innocence in that bar to Eddie, I would guess, though I never saw what they did. He was a seedy, low-life character with no spine. I didn't trust him at all; later I would be right to have felt that way.

He stood first in line to bad-mouth my father, once his business partner and drinking companion. Blood and violence were a part of my father's life. I was desensitized to it then; I ignored it, surrounding myself with pretty things. Eventually, it got to me though, and I found myself less the sweet girl I wanted to be.

My father loved to fight. He was like a pit bull—once they tasted blood, they looked for it again and again. He raised my brother to be the same way.

Once, when my brother was about nine, a stronger, bigger boy of fourteen challenged him, calling him names and insulting our mother. My father was sleeping because our restaurants were open twenty-four hours, and he worked the night shifts. When Daddy heard the commotion outside, he told my brother that if he didn't kick the kid's ass, he, my father, would kick his, my brother's. So my brother kicked the older kid's ass, and no one from that day on could look at him wrong.

I don't recall many stories that my father told that didn't include some fighting in them. He was a tough guy who was thrown out of school and beaten by the nuns. He lifted weights and got fit at boot camp during the Korean War, and that bad-boy image stayed with him. Somehow, it suited him. He had a sexy face and bad-boy baby-blues, so he got away with—well, they say, murder.

One of my favorite memories is when I was about twelve, and we lived in our red house on South Road. Daddy brought home a canvas laundry bag filled with money—I mean a big laundry bag, the kind your kids bring home from college. He dumped it on the bed, showed me how to stack the bills by currency and seals, and left to take a shower, glancing once over his shoulder to wink and say, "It was a good day for selling hamburgers, huh?"

Have you ever seen a $1,000 bill that wasn't from a Monopoly game? I have; I saw lots of them. I counted and sorted cash for hours. It was thrilling and scary, and I had no idea where it came from. I trusted him when I was young—at least until I found out he was cheating on us. Still, he taught me how to play liars' poker that day with those piles of bills, and I became a serious adversary.

During the earliest dates with my husband, I hustled him pretty badly. Thankfully, I didn't inherit any of Daddy's other habits.

I drove my father to meetings quite a bit once I was legally able; actually, he let me drive when I was fifteen, before I had a permit. The luncheons consisted of me reading a Harold Robbins book while eating a tomato stuffed with tuna fish, or some kind of salad. Daddy had dealings with men that stepped off the screen of *Goodfellows* and *Donnie Brasco*; none of them had the class of *The Godfather*.

In the end, Dad was set up; I was at that meeting too. According to the articles I have retained in my files, he was the eastern Suffolk County representative of the Joseph Columbo organized crime family. He was arrested and jumped bail. It is interesting to note that he was arrested in New York, posted a huge amount for bail, was allowed to travel out of the state to his second home in Florida, and was last seen at a meeting with a known Mob figure.

Later, this Mob guy showed up at the mirror shop my father was a partner in, demanding to know where my father was. My father's partners at the time paid a heavy price for his disappearance;

28

there certainly is another book, much juicer and more Mafia-like there. I hope to have the privilege of co-writing that one with his now-deceased partner's wife.

After dad left, I was in the dark. Nothing made sense. All my efforts to get at the facts were thwarted. Even when I tried to hire a private investigator, Phil, he said it was a cut-and-dried case; my father went down as the fall guy. The happenings, articles, and stories relayed to me many years later didn't jibe with that scenario.

One article about the set up said this guy, Richard Annicharico, who arranged with my father to save his own ass after he was caught by the IRS, said Daddy was the guilty one.

Richard was a bad-actor type—you know, "How you doin'?" wink, smile, nudge. He was sweaty and fidgety while doing his best "Joey" from *Friends*. No contest there. My intuition was right on; the guy was all wrong. He studied me, engaging me in conversation, though my father thwarted his efforts.

At similar meetings, I was paid little interest beyond a greeting, and these men assured my father of my beauty, my resemblance to him, and, perhaps, an inquiry of my brother. Their detached posture left little room for suspicion. In contrast, Mr. Double Agent prolonged our lunch, which was set at a round table large enough for eight, which was also weird. Usually, we had a booth in the back; today they were all taken, and he was waiting at the table for us.

The first time I saw *The Godfather*, many years after it came out, I shuddered at the scene I had been a character in. The waiter also paid a lot of attention to us; he was probably an agent, too. I remember my father leaning in to this guy to talk in those hushed tones, and "Uncool Anthony" smiling at me, nervous and uncomfortable. Previously, I'd paid little attention when I drove my dad, finding the lunches uneventful and dutifully attended. Most of the men gave me the creeps.

On this day, I had no book, so I brought the new *Cosmopolitan* with me. I felt edgy with this guy, as though he were looking through my clothes. As it turned out, he was. His dealings with my father were taped and photographed, which is why I became so interesting to the agencies looking for him. I saved all of the business cards and articles I could find, but I still don't know the truth.

As I write this, it may sound as though I thought my father was a good guy and shouldn't have been caught. I'm not naïve. I know he was capable of killing; he was a soldier. Naturally, I wish he had gone straight and done his time, and that things had been different. What irked me was that this guy, this crook in his own right who was caught in his scam, got to be free because he set my father up, and my father took a big, big fall.

Daddy thought he was untouchable. He thought he was so smart—too smart. We all did. He studied the "Japs," as he called them, in the Korean War. He said they were "the sneakiest people on earth; they'll stab you in the back while you're pissing in the wind." He studied his enemies, and kept them close.

I think he was blindsided. He thought he had worth, that his people would take care of him. If it's true that he is dead, then I guess they did. That's where we had something in common; we thought we, his kids, were his people and that he would take care of us like he'd promised.

I never believed he was dead; I couldn't feel it. After his arrest, he was scared, his ex said, but the truth was he looked out for Number One, and that was him. I have articles with quotes from Mob members stating he was not hit (killed); otherwise, the guy that disappeared at the same time as him would not be in hiding too, and "it would be on the street".

There were sightings of him, too, and, supposedly, he went to the school of my half brother. After my father disappeared, a lot of people he had been in contact with, like Scavelli and Rego, testified against Daddy. Neil was a phony who flirted and hit on my mother—a really creepy character.

He is probably the mayor by now; that's usually how it works. He and the others profited from the "unsavory snake-type" character, as Neil called my dad in the papers. They pointed the finger at him, disengage themselves from any and all connections. These men are cowards.

Years later, I ran into Mr. Rego, and a friend reintroduced us. He must have thought I was ashamed of my father and impressed with his prosperity, that I would think well of him; it seemed important to him that I did. But I know how he got started; his hands are dirty, too. For as many people that Daddy helped on their way up the ladder—the ones remaining with enough skeletons in their closets to open a museum—he hurt a lot of people on the way down, too. I was left to face these people, snubbed and embarrassed by their contempt and lies. Harassed and attacked, I was the last one standing in that town after his fall—a young woman, an innocent person, left holding a fireball.

After Valentines Day in 1980, when I went to Florida as Daddy instructed me to—I was in New York at the time—his girlfriend was not comfortable with my being there. Thank God for Kathy, the young woman who lived upstairs from us. She took me in, lent me her car, and got me a job; she was the mother and comforter I hungered, though she is not much older than I. We had a blast; she helped me heal as much as I could at the time, and forever we have been friends because of that time.

I tracked down "Umus" fifteen years later; another person who lied and stole from us; she said that my father was scared and sorry. She and "Uncle Larry," the molester, maintained that nothing was left from my father's home. When I showed up at her house— voilà—all of Daddy's furniture relaxed in her living room.

Uncle Larry had our personal belongings, including all our photographs and my brother's letter jacket, (which he still has). They all lied and stole from us; they abandoned us when we needed family, and then hid out like they were protecting themselves. Umus was the one girlfriend I trusted, and she turned out to be sneakier and a bigger thief than the others. To her defense, she was a scared, young mother; in her heart I know that she knows my father would have been disappointed in her rejection of us, and a further reason to break up the family.

I spoke to Daddy on that last day—his last, supposedly. He instructed me on the phone to call Ed Scavelli, who would give me the money for a ticket, and that I should stay with Umus and Matthew, my ½ brother Eddie didn't want to give me the $66, and asked me how or when I would pay it back. Umus couldn't bear to have me there. She told me she needed privacy and time to think, so I moved in with Kathy upstairs.

I was really messed up and confused. I stayed until the spring, when I could secure work and residence in New York. I went back believing that dear, sweet Umus would keep in touch and let me know when she would move so that I could get the belongings of my father, which we were entitled to. Instead, she had the phones disconnected, and I never heard from her again. I will grant her the benefit of being scared for her child's safety from the people who may be interested in him, but the truth is that she lied and stole, and she took away the half brother I loved.

I am certain that Daddy hurt himself irreparably, having to leave his entire family behind. Whatever his fate, it was not worse than living without the opportunity to benefit from the empty promises he made to us—his children, and his wife. To live in a riddle for twenty-three years has been a heavy sentence for loving someone unconditionally.

We weren't the only ones who got screwed. As I mentioned earlier, his last partners at Mira Mar Glass in Florida became targets; fear, harassment, violence, and liability for his debts were their inheritance for loving and trusting Daddy, too. Umus continued to work there as well, and she, too, became an enemy to those good people.

It seems that he never paid the taxes from the business, either. The crazy thing is that everyone trusted his cons. His lifestyle was kind of glamorous, especially in the early '70s. His ex-partners wound up in a lot of trouble. One of them became a drug dealer to pay the taxes my father was "taking care of." He kidnapped someone and wound up doing jail time.

During this time, I was running full speed on a treadmill, going nowhere fast. I had no moral compass, and I didn't want to feel anything. Fear is paralyzing, but I didn't know I was living in it. I didn't know a lot of stuff.

I have few memories of family times with Daddy, especially enjoyable ones. The ones I cherish were Sunday dinners when my mother would make lasagna, stuffed shells, or manicotti for as many as twenty people. Often, this was when I got to spend time with him, sitting on his lap as his pet. He adored my mother's cooking, and early on, I saw that it would be the perfect arrow to pierce his heart and lure men to me.

My first effort was cooking for the wrestling team during my sophomore year, and after that, I had my standing—even though my brother forbade me to date any of them. I had a hard time getting dates in high school; I thought it was me, and I admit to feeling relief years later when I found out my father's reputation in the community had something to do with it.

My father sang to me *"A Pretty Girl is Like a Melody."* I was his princess—his pretty baby. None of this bothered me, because it was all I knew. The only other friend I had with a father who paid attention to her was Geraldine, and she had to share him with her siblings. So unless I watched *Father Knows Best*, I didn't feel slighted. I did feel odd, though, and I worked hard for many years to gain the admiration and love of those people I wanted to be a part of, to feel like I was just living a regular kid's life. I wanted to be normal, though I know now "normal" has a wide range of reality.

When we moved to West Hampton Beach, I was in the second grade. That year I began having a nightmare that lasted half of my life: My mother, brother, and I are inside our house on South Road playing Monopoly. A black limousine screeches into the driveway, bottoming out when it hits the huge pothole at the center of the drive. We stand to look out of the large bay window to see who pulled up. The passenger doors on the right side open simultaneously, exposing three men, one of whose hands are tied behind his back, his white shirt torn and stained with blood, is dragged toward the house. The screaming man yells and warns before he is whacked in the mouth and ribs over and over. One man holds a hand gun to the bound man's head, while the other approaches our front door with a machine gun.

The sun falls slowly behind them, bathing them in orange light. The smell of freshly washed grass stings my nostrils. A panic seizes our mother, who pulls us toward a closet we used for linens. She tucks us into its deep shelves, pulling the linens over us while she huddles under us on the floor, a heavy down comforter pulled tightly around her. We hear the door bang open and our father's haunted cries. These goons bellow, "You're gonna watch me blow the wife and kiddies away if you don't do what we say," his ugly baritone voice rasps. The noise rips through my ears, devouring my consciousness, as bullets fly by my head, arms, and legs.

It is the daunting silence that wakes me every time, making me shudder in my bed.

I had that dream until I was twenty-two years old, when my father disappeared. Somehow I knew then, that although I had no idea what organized crime was, my father lived a duality that would fracture our existence.

Last week, we got bedroom furniture delivered. I had to put my stuff in boxes so we could get rid of the old furniture. I found some teeth in a silver box scrolled with tiny hearts and leaves etched into it. The teeth belonged to my dog, Rja. I rescued her from the pound when I came to California in 1980, when I realized that Daddy wasn't coming back and I was potentially in danger alone in New York.

I held those baby teeth in my hands and fantasized what it would feel like if someone were to call me and tell me they identified my father by his dental records. I used to create elaborate deaths for him in my mind, and sometimes on paper, so I could feel the relief of an end.

I took out the papers I'd collected through the years of his absence—articles and phone numbers for people who were no longer there. It made me a little crazy again, so I got on line and tried a few Web sites that had the word "mafia" in them. I went into the FBI site and tried to get into their archives, to no avail. Then I e-mailed some people who write about the Mafia, asking where I could obtain some more information. This book has befuddled me; in the efforts I have taken to seek a closure, I keep opening wounds. But they're not as painful. I'm just hungry now, like a researcher.

Time has moved me forward—sometimes slowly, other times rushing me into experiences that left me breathless. I needed a strong moral figure in my life, but I didn't have one. I kept trying to tap into a way to become one for myself. I volunteered with kids and raised money for charities. I even went to homeless shelters. I took in lots of stray people and tried to give my boys the fibers of humanity at all levels. In an effort to grasp this gold ring I felt robbed of, I put myself out there to be a vessel for whatever good I could do.

Today, I am a mentor for teenage girls. It feels good to have a hand in directing them; I sure could have used one when I was growing up. It amazes me that they aren't little homemakers like I was when I was their ages. I had the responsibility of the house most of the time. My mother was working two or three jobs most of the time, and I am kind of a clean person. I don't do well in chaos; I need things organized, though I am far from anal.

I decided to begin a sort of training for my girls to help them learn some cooking skills—a few meals and other lessons in home economics. I have two girls, Heather and Katie. I worked with a non-profit organization I helped to organize called Serenity Village for Women. We created Serenity Sisters, hence the mentoring.

My girls are at an age now that they don't really need me every day; like my own teenage son, they are struggling for their independence— their identity. So, I let them know through e-mail, cards, and calls that I am here. Katie lives on my street, so I see her almost every day. Though she is on a path that has her walking the opposite way from me, I know that she knows I am here. I was appalled that, unlike Heather, Katie could not cook to save her life. So, we set up an appointment to shop and prepare a meal. Katie chose lasagna because she likes it. Here is the recipe for Lasagna:

≈

Lasagna – Sauce

1 can crushed tomatoes (Progresso)

1 small can tomato paste

1 can tomato puree (28 oz.)

1 onion (sweet), chopped

1 cup chopped celery

1 clove garlic, minced

Garlic salt to taste

Dash oregano

light olive oil-enough to line pan-approx ¼ cup

Fresh parsley

Italian seasonings to taste

1 pkg. lasagna noodles

Stuffing for Lasagna or Stuffed Shells

1-2 lbs. ground sirloin

32 ounces ricotta cheese (whole milk if possible)

16 ounces mozzarella cheese

1 bag washed baby spinach

Garlic salt or salt (to taste)

Celery salt or powder

Lemon pepper

Parmesan cheese to taste (use a good grade of cheese)

Fresh parsley- chopped fine (wash 1/2 bunch)

Whether I am making a quick sauce like this or from fresh tomatoes, I start the same way. In a large saucepan, I put the olive oil, minced garlic rubbed around on the bottom of the pan, and the onions, celery, oregano, a pinch of salt, and any other Italian seasonings you like. (I add a small amount of fresh basil because it can take over the taste of the sauce, which you may like.) Let them begin to simmer, then add chopped parsley. After the onions and celery look soft, I add the crushed tomatoes (Fresh tomatoes are a different story; e-mail me for changes) and the puree or paste if you prefer it. Bring this to a very slow boil, and then cover and simmer, stirring so it doesn't stick to the bottom.

Put a large pot of water with 2 tablespoons of vegetable oil and a tablespoon of salt to boil on the stove. Slice a large chunk of mozzarella cheese (whole milk if you can) about ¼" thick onto a plate and refrigerate for later.

In another pan, I prepare the stuffing for the lasagna or shells, if you prefer. I use ground sirloin because it has little fat and a better flavor. To the ground sirloin, add garlic salt, celery salt, and lemon pepper to taste—I find ½ teaspoon of each works nicely, though I do add a little of each after the cheeses are blended together with the meat. Lightly brown, then add cleaned, stemmed spinach to the beef mixture. Let it wilt without allowing it to disintegrate. When mixture is cooked (not overcooked), remove, and with a slotted spoon, transfer from pan to bowl to remove excess oil from meat. Set aside.

When mixture is cooled to room temperature, add the ricotta cheese, the Parmesan (fresh Parmesan can be purchased in the deli section) and ½ the mozzarella; put the other half aside. With rubber spoon, blend together. Refrigerate stuffing. Heat oven to 375 degrees. I spray each uncooked piece of lasagna with a vegetable spray before I place it into the water so that it doesn't stick. Allow to boil approximately 12 minutes. It is okay if the noodles are not completely cooked, as they will cook in the oven. Remove the cooked noodles, and run under cold water while separating as best as you can.

In a glass (if you have one) baking dish, large enough to accommodate the noodles, lightly spray the sides and bottoms of dish with vegetable spray. I prefer 13-by-9-by-2 Pyrex. Layer the bottom of dish with tomato sauce, be generous (not too), then layer noodles on sauce. I use 3 or 4 noodles so it is easier to serve. Then, spoon the chesses/spinach on top. Spinach is optional. Gently spread the cheeses mixture ***TIP: (I use my hands), and add another layer of sauce, then a layer of noodles, until the ingredients are gone. I use a bag of shredded mozzarella on top after the last layer of sauce so it serves easier and looks nicer.

The oven should be heated to 375. Cover dish with foil after inserting toothpicks so the cheese won't stick to the foil. Cook covered for 15 minutes; uncover, and cook until sauce is lightly bubbling and cheese is melted. If your pan is very full, place a piece of foil under the second rack to catch the drippings.

This dish takes about an hour to prepare and cook, especially if you have helpers for chopping and cutting. The girls enjoy the prep work, and so do my boys!

This dish is highlighted with a light salad and bread if you are interested. I serve a light wine—red/white or Chianti.

LAYER 2

The Title Party—What's in a Name?

"All glory comes from daring to begin."

Anonymous

While completing this book, I mentioned to my life coach, Deb, my frustration and inability to think of a title that resonated with my intentions and sentiments. Usually, I am full of titles, but I could not decide how I wanted to present this book; what genre could it be classified as? Deb suggested that I read a book by Susan Page, *The Shortest Distance Between You and a Published Book.* Susan introduced steps to finding a good title, which is essential for the success of any written piece. One of her suggestions was to have a "title" party. Once I read that, I didn't even finish the chapter (not until later).

That's it, I thought; I could create the last recipe and a title by throwing a party—my favorite thing. I told Deb and set the date for June 24, 2001. I was uneasy releasing copies of the unfinished, unedited, untitled culmination of my words and recipes. (I couldn't bring myself to call it a book.) I felt naked, but Deb was there to support me and talk me through it, and my husband said to go for it. Even my kids were encouraging; they asked me about the progress, and my oldest son kept asking to read it. This terrified me, but I prayed a lot and kept going; I knew if I didn't, I'd suffer, and my kids would not gain a lesson in confidence that I could give them by my own experience.

To say I felt like a charlatan—"I declare myself an author"—felt like a swindle. I was terrified. I assured myself that these were people that liked—even loved—me, and I mailed copies to the guests on the list; I knew if I didn't, I would agonize, wondering, "What if?" I figured if it was a bust, I succeeded because I tried.

Moving forward, I purchased three ring binders, enclosed copies of the pages I'd written, wrote a letter of explanation and request for help, and said a prayer; I would remain open to the experience.

The first copy I sent out was to Donna Marie. We've been cohorts and friends forever. Donna is an elementary school teacher—the kind you wish you had had and pray that your children get. I figured if she could get through it, I would be okay. When the phone rang the next day, it was Donna, raving and praising my work.

I was genuinely taken aback. I am always surprised when I am praised for my writing. I kept waiting for the admonishment about grammar, tenses, and spelling, because this was seriously raw material—first draft stuff—but it didn't come. Our phone kept ringing; everyone who read it had marvelous things to say, and they couldn't wait for the party! I am not naïve; I know my friends were repressing suggestions and comments—criticisms even—but they were interested in supporting me first; my fragility was on their minds. I will forever be grateful for their openness and support; they bolstered my courage.

Favorable support continued to cheer me. My friend Ron said, "No offense, but I can't believe this came from you." He has a way with words; still, negative repression replaced itself with positive thoughts.

The morning of the 24th, I awoke at 6 a.m. to the sound of finches bathing in my fountain. I dressed for my daily walk. I had been training for the Avon 3-Day Walk for breast and ovarian cancer since March and had a regime that I never deviated from. On August 8, I would fly to Seattle to walk sixty miles in three days with thousands of people. After Patti, my mother-in-law, passed from cancer, I felt this walk was something I needed to do to bring the remaining tendrils of my grief to rest on the roads my feet travel. So I put on my headset and cranked up Barry White, whose moaning and gyrating walked me mile after mile. I had been walking at least eight miles a day since May. My feet became the vehicle for my aching heart to heal and thoughts of the title party to take form.

Full of spunk, I moved faster and harder toward the end of my walk. Suddenly, I felt a sharp, familiar pain; I had thrown my back out and though I tried to walk it off, I just couldn't. Crying with frustration, I had to have my husband come pick me up. At home, I climbed into our spa and soaked for half an hour. I showered, dressed, took 800 milligrams of Motrin, put my ice pack on my seat and drove to Santa Monica Seafood in Newport. I kept my mind occupied on the dinner and what I was going to purchase.

It was a clear, cloudless day. The familiar smells of the market drove my appetite; I chose small, black mussels (East Coast mussels are my favorite), large, raw shrimp, clam juice, and fresh dinner rolls. I had the clerk put ice in plastic bags to pack around the mussels and shrimp so they would stay cold while I was picking up my friend Rosemary from the airport. She had extended her stay in California so she could attend the party. I am so blessed.

I got to the airport in plenty of time and walked around to stretch my back. After a while, it dawned on me that I was looking at the wrong flight because she had given me a specific time, and the two did not coincide. When I went to the counter and inquired, I was told there was no flight from San Francisco at that time. I decided to have her paged in case she was at another airline or gate, though I was assured no flight had come in that gate. When Rosemary answered her page, I discovered she had been sitting in the row right behind where I had settled for twenty minutes waiting for the flight that had not arrived. Go figure.

Rosemary was tired from her weekend, and I was hurting, but being together gave us the lift we needed to move us forward. For me, there is nothing more invigorating than being with my friends—especially Rosemary, whom I call Scrosie.

At home, my husband was working hard. He is the best partner; I am beyond lucky to have him. Although I knew Scrosie was ready for a nap, she jumped right in, helping set up tables. I went inside to survey my purchases and begin food preparations.

I had gone to the Farmer's Market on Friday and purchased fresh fruits and veggies. I couldn't decide how elaborate a meal I would create, or even what exactly it would be, until that moment my other self took over. I am fearless in the kitchen.

Chopping and preparing gets me going; it's my warm-up. I confess that I never know if my creation will be enjoyed. I wing it, cross my fingers, and say a prayer. I am not always successful, but I put forth my best effort based purely on instinct. I used to think the great chefs were a hit every time, but it's not so. Sometimes they make a meal look beautiful or exotic, which stimulates your other senses and fools your taste buds. They are merely tricks of the trade. Never be afraid to make something different; that is how new recipes are created!

I decided I would prepare mussels and shrimp sautéed with fresh vegetables over penne pasta. A few of my guests were vegans, and I knew I could alter the dish easily. I also prepared a side dish of ratatouille six hours in advance. Ratatouille reminds me of my friend Pierre, whose rendition was prepared in the style of his French-Algerian ancestors and was delicious. My recipe is borrowed from a cookbook. I had purchased some wonderful greens, tomatoes and other exotic, seasonal vegetables to create a colorful salad. I prepared the salad and stored it in the fridge with a wet, wrung-out towel on top to keep it crisp. I never put the dressing on the salad until we are sitting down.

Two hours before I served dinner, I prepared Hot Mint Malt to serve instead of coffee or tea afterward. It is wise to do as much food preparation in advance as possible; this early planning allows for time to focus on the delicate details. A good way to store individual ingredients is to separate them into several small, glass bowls. You will not have to search for anything while creating dishes in front of guests. This method works very nicely, and it looks professional, too.

Dessert was still a mystery. I didn't want to serve cakes or pies that needed cutting; I wanted something simple, elegant, and yummy. In the end, I drove to a bakery and chose petite pastries to compliment the fresh strawberries from the Farmer's Market.

***TIP: The grower at the Farmer's Market showed me his method for determining a sweet strawberry: Lift the stem away from the fruit, and if it is tight and shiny around the top of the berry but not mushy, it will be sweet and ripe. He was absolutely right!

Since I wanted this dinner to be elegant and comfortable, I spared no details. I rented several items for my party—china, crystal, silver and a double-burner stovetop so I could cook outside in front of my guests. I chose magenta and ceylon for the rented table linens that would cover two fifty-four-inch round tables surrounded by sixteen gold, straight-back chairs. Rosemary and I set the tables, placing fresh flowers and votive candles around the yard for lighting and ambiance. I am a candle fanatic; ask anyone who's dined at our home. I have been known to start a fire or two. Traci, my neighbor/friend makes it her mission to keep an eye on the candles, as does my niece Laurie. Laurie was here for the Christmas the fireplace caught fire; in her young, timid voice, she said, "Aunt Lu, the fireplace is on fire."

The candles were in glass votives set in glass coasters away from all flammable objects. I was concerned that the wisteria covering our patio would drop leaves in the food, so I purchased gold tulle at Wal-Mart for ninety-nine cents per yard and draped it horizontally from one side of the patio cover to the other, securing it with a staple gun. My husband is expert at such ideas and strong—and he looks sexy on a ladder. Before the netting was fastened, we hung delicate, pearly lights across the patio cover underneath, creating a wistful effect. I have a small yard, but with a little imagination and help, it has been transformed into many thematic settings.

Everything came together nicely, and I was having that feeling I get before I entertain; I tingle from the inside as though I had swallowed fairy dust, which tells me all will go well. But, as with all planning, things can go wrong. If they do, don't panic; be flexible, just as you would if you didn't have an ingredient for a recipe; that's how new recipes are created!

While wiping the delicate, glass bowls to float my gardenias in, I accidentally put my finger through one of them. Uninjured, I went looking for a store that was still open to find something else for centerpieces because the size of the tables and the height of my vases did not mesh. At 6 p.m., I found two handmade fuchsia flowers whose cup centers held a candle. Thank God for Willow Manor. It was not what I planned but I was happy with the result.

After the patio was set up, I showered. I still didn't know what I would wear, but I felt confident that the right attire would show itself to me, and—*voilà*— an unworn dress fell off a hanger, landing at my feet! In twenty minutes, I was dressed. I have learned that if I spend too much time dressing and prepping myself, I am unhappy with the finished product and am usually uncomfortable.

My mother arrived, and I put her to work. She was such a gem; before, during, and after the party, she performed a number of tasks—some tedious and unpleasant. We have not lived in the same state or city for some time, so it was extra special to have her there. She even came over early that day and washed my windows when the window washer flaked out on me! There are a million tiny blessings everywhere you look if you are open to them; make it a mantra.

I continued preparations: cutting Genoa hard salami, three cheeses I had never tasted before, and fresh veggies with sour cream dips from the packets. I didn't want everyone to fill up on appetizers or too much alcohol, so I limited both.

My guests arrived promptly, except Ron, who always makes an entrance. It was exciting introducing these friends, each a gem, to one another; it's strange to think how each of these people is in my life, and, until this night, my husband hadn't met some of them.

By the time I got everything ready for my dinner, I felt like I should be on the food channel or something. It was dark, and we had to add candles to my cooking table so I could see better, but it didn't help much. I figured that as many meals as I've cooked, I could do it in the dark. I was pleased to see several half-eaten plates when I took my seat.

I still had no idea where this particular journey would escort me. Through my life's voyage, I've become aware that all excursions are equipped with a destination, though they often lack a traditional map. A willingness to savor the juices in the bottom of the pan or to go where the journey takes you is half the excitement. I recommend some passage without predetermined destinations; it keeps life tasty.

A recipe is a set of instructions for preparing an intention—one method of attaining a desired end or goal— and often, the objective is unknown. In my life, the combination of people, places, and purpose has become the ingredients inspiring my brand of Heirloom Rituals; writing about it made it real.

Acknowledging me has taken time. I believed I had a path. Traveling the road of instinct, I'd get a notion, which I'd develop into an intention. Sometimes I'd create an edible way to serve it; sometimes I'd just write about it and leave it. Either way, it has brought me closer to self-realization; I am simply me. I feared that I lacked the ability to perform a tangible service that I could expand upon to make a contribution to my world—to my family. I felt deficient.

I realize now, I contribute every day; whether anyone knows of my offerings, they still happen. That has to be enough, or I never will be enough to myself. What an arrogant assumption to think my will could eclipse God's, that whatever gifts I've been given, I thought I knew better. I am perfecting those contributions; it's the least I can do to be thankful for all I have been given. Exploring this path—lover of life, people, food, ritual, writing, and journey—has freed me for my next venture, the mysteries of my unknown.

The title party proved to be the perfect demonstration of my book's intent. Writing, cooking, and gathering, my harvest shared under the canopy of my wisteria tree, brought identity to my chapters, linking them toward a binding. I accepted that publishing this book myself might not carry the prestige of being picked up by a publisher or agent. In fact, I put forth every effort to serve my book's intentions to agents and publishers—a difficult task, since they require a synopsis in one sentence and are hard pressed to read on if they don't get it right off. I saved every rejection—fifty-two— because it is a part of my process. I realize that an unknown writer such as myself has no carrot to dangle in front of these elite selectors of literary menus. So, in an effort to present my work my way, I will pay for my process if only to have it come full circle. I would be lying if I said I didn't want to sell this book, but more importantly, I want to see it to fruition so I can say that I did it myself. I am in control in as much as that means surrendering my will to the highest power of all.

I had no experience in titling a book. I couldn't answer the questions publishers asked according to Susan Page's book. Where would you see this book in the bookstore? How would it be packaged? What makes your book different than those on the shelf, and why should we buy it? I had no idea; therefore, in an effort to manufacture a savvy stance, I took a leap of faith with my process and came out a winner before my product was complete.

My friends applauded me as though I were a professional writer, published and successful. My guests' input for title suggestions were too numerous to choose just one. They were entertaining and heartwarming. My husband gave a speech—words of love and pride about this woman who was emerging in the clothes of his wife. Rosemary, my own personal Tinkerbell, portrayed her version of Vanna White, copying each title on the easel pad my husband provided with drama and style. My mother beamed with pride. My friends helped in every way. Traci and Derek took on the roles of co-host and hostess out of love and faith in my endeavors. My coach sent me vibes of pride and positive energy. LaurieAnn and Carrie, who edited, supported, and cheered me on, united in their belief in me.

Every guest and every supporter unable to be there sent me unconditional love. Ron documented the evening by photographing each momentous moment until I blushed. In one evening, I received more gifts than I ever dreamed. The titles were creative, funny, and heartfelt; more than eighteen months later, I still hadn't chosen a title. Then one day, my oldest son answered the phone and told the caller, "My mom can't come to the phone; she's giving lessons in lasagna." Then he hung up and said, "Mom, that should be your title."

The success of my party far exceeded finding a title. The pouring of great minds and miracles into the little vessel that is *me* gifted me with clarification. I recognize people, me included, have hunger pangs far deeper than food can suppress. I see that by feeding the stomach, I feed the soul; by writing my feelings down, I made sense of them. I am loved; it's that basic.

On my Web site under Title Party are the titles from the party and some photos. Tell me which title you would have chosen, or if after reading the book you think my son was right, by e-mailing me at madamelu@pacbell.net. Thanks!

≈

Recipe for Black Mussels, Shrimp, and Penne Primavera

2 pounds Penne Pasta (Boil the water while you are chopping and add a pinch of salt. Cook the pasta; drain, add olive oil and a sprinkle of salt. Cover, stirring occasionally to keep from sticking.)

4 pounds of black mussels ***TIP (Choose the smallest mussels; they are sweeter and more tender. Also never accept any mollusks if they are open, even a little. You could get sick if they were not properly chilled.)

3 pounds large, raw shrimp

6 ripe tomatoes if large; 9 if plum or small

1 bunch shallots

4 stalks celery

3 cloves garlic sliced thinly

2 zucchini

1 head cauliflower

1 small bunch broccoli

1 cup sugar snap peas

1 can water chestnuts

1 cup fresh spinach (I lightly sauté the spinach in some lemon juice, before adding it to the pot, I use kitchen scissors to cut it into small pieces.)

½ cup soaked pine nuts (Prior to eating, soak nuts for 6 to 8 hours; it takes a lot of the fat out and makes them absorb the flavor of the oil and seasonings better.)

Olive oil as needed

Fresh basil to taste

Fresh oregano (cut) to taste

Salt and pepper to taste

Bunch fresh parsley (Sauté with spinach.)

Sun-dried tomato spread to taste (I use 2 heaping tablespoons.)

1 jar artichoke hearts (Save some of the juice.)

3 tablespoons capers with juice

1 bottle clam juice

1 cup white wine

I had all these ingredients prearranged in dishes and available to me on a prep table I set up beside the burner. I used my largest and deepest frying pan, but a saucepan would work, too. Toss and serve salad and wine; leave open bottles on the table.

I poured about 3 tablespoons of olive oil into the pot and added the shallots, celery, garlic, oregano, basil, salt, pepper, white wine, pine nuts, and tomato, spread to sauté. I stirred it occasionally while explaining to my guests what I was doing. Once the ingredients were slightly softened, I added the chopped tomatoes. These tomatoes were tender and sweet, so I left the skins on. If the skins are tough, remove them by dropping them into boiling water for a minute or two, then into a bowl of cold water. The skins should peel off easily.

***TIP: If tomatoes are not in season, substitute with two cans of chopped tomatoes—preferably Progresso, but any will do.

I let the tomatoes come to a light simmer, then added parsley/ spinach mixture.

To create a sumptuous foundation in which to enfold your vegetables and seafood, keep the sauce light. If the stock is bubbling rapidly, turn down the flame and add the remaining vegetables except the artichokes, capers, and snap peas. Too much heat will reduce the liquid base.

***TIP: I lightly steamed the broccoli and cauliflower for a few minutes before so they will not have to cook long in the pan.

While I was cooking the vegetables, my guests were getting rowdy and asking for the next step, which they could barely see because I had not provided enough light in my cooking area. I laughed and enjoyed the secrecy as though I were a mad scientist. I sipped on Calloway Sauvignon Blanc (I used it in the recipe, too) while my vegetables absorbed the flavors in the pan. I added the shrimp about five minutes later and covered the pan for two minutes to create steam. Then, I added the clam juice, mussels, and snap peas, and stirred the mixture gently but continuously. I added the remainder of ingredients just before serving, leaving a few minutes for ingredients to blend in pan.

The preparation time was under 20 minutes. Take care not to overcook.

***TIP: Here are a few more tips: Stir a tablespoon of olive oil per pound of warming pasta to keep it from sticking together.

***TIP: I heated my oven to about 200 degrees twenty minutes before serving time. I turned off the oven, then placed plates on the top rack. (Make sure the plates are oven-safe.) I positioned pasta onto plates, then placed the seafood on top of the pasta in a decorative fashion. While you are filling plates, choose assistants. I had my lovely helpers, Traci and Derek, serving for me with their personal panache and style.

The bread came out of the oven at the perfect time. (I always assign a guest to bread duty so I don't forget and burn it.) Lovely toasts were made, and the sounds of satisfied palates filled my ears.

≈

Simple Light Salad Dressing

½-¾ cup olive oil (Use a light-tasting one unless you like the heavier taste of olives.)

½ -¼ cup balsamic vinegar

2 tablespoons rice vinegar or red wine, if you prefer

2 teaspoons fresh chopped mint

1 teaspoon garlic salt

1 teaspoon lemon pepper

3 tablespoons lime juice (preferably fresh squeezed)

Mix ingredients in bottle or bowl; shake or whisk vigorously before pouring over salad. Serve immediately.

Makes about four cups and perfectly serves 20 people as a side dish

≈

Party-Style Ratatouille (Mable Hoffman's Crockery Cooking)

1 medium eggplant, peeled and finely chopped

1 zucchini, chopped

¼ - ½ cup sun-dried tomatoes in oil, drained and chopped

1 yellow bell pepper, finely chopped

1 medium red onion, finely chopped

1 clove garlic, crushed

1 cup chopped fresh cilantro

3 tablespoons olive oil

2 tablespoons white wine vinegar

Salt to taste

Pepper to taste

Combine all ingredients in a slow cooker. Cover and cook on low for 6 to 7 hours or until tender. Serve hot.

Hot Mint Malt (Mable Hoffman's Crockery Cooking)

Doubled, makes 20 demitasse cups

3-8 chocolate-covered, cream-filled mint patties, 1½ inches in diameter. (I couldn't find these, so I used a pound of bulk candy and it worked fine)

10 cups milk

1 cup malted milk powder

2 teaspoons vanilla extract

Whipped cream

In a slow cooker, combine mint patties, milk, malted powder and vanilla. Cover and heat on low heat for 2 hours. Beat with a rotary beater until frothy. Pour into cups; top with whipped cream.

*** TIP: Use Demitasse cups; this beverage is rich.

I laid out the desserts and strawberries for self-service. The crock pot with the malt was also set on the table for self-service. I wanted interaction with my guests after we ate. Everyone gathered around the dessert table and chatted. I removed my apron—a gift from my son—and surveyed my surroundings. The candles flickered as they reached the ends of their wicks. I felt the joy one experiences when someone likes a gift you chose with care. Stars filled the sky as well as my back yard. My children came home, timidly approaching me, their mom. They stood on either side of my husband and me, and I thought, "I am a happy, fortunate woman."

With desserts in hands, we reconvened for the title presentation, which was entertaining and enlightening. The responses were interesting, charming, sentimental and funny, as well as poignant. As the evening drew to a close, I knew it was an experience I would cherish always. Love and friendships are the taste buds of the heart.

LAYER 3

Lobster, Lucia, and Sir Richard Burton

"All of us should eat and drink and enjoy what we have worked
for. It is God's gift."

Ecclesiastes 3:13

For my sixteenth birthday, my mother invited me to dinner at our favorite restaurant, René's Caso Baso in Westhampton, N.Y. René's illustrious career as a gourmet chef and restaurateur created an elegant place to relax, eat, and be pampered. René would regale us with his stories of Italy and the war. He waited on Hitler and Mussolini! Perhaps he'll dictate his book to me one day.

He was a dear, sweet man who lost his youngest daughter, Nadine, who was also my friend and schoolmate in junior high.

Nadine was a lovely, petite girl, filled with life. She went on a school trip to Europe and contracted some type of upper respiratory infection that filled her lungs with fluid and drowned her. I am writing this to the best of my recollection. Her funeral stands out in my mind though, many, many people gathered in shock on frigid, barren ground to bury this family's sunshine. It was tragic, and it dimmed the light in René's eyes.

The summer is wild in the Hamptons; it has been a stomping ground for the rich and famous for as long as I can remember. Though I was never what you would call privileged, my parents, as restaurant/bar owners, had carved out a celebrity that afforded us a certain amount of red-carpet treatment. We were seated in the front of the restaurant, near the door, one table away from our usual spot, which was occupied by three men. At first glance I did not recognize the very intoxicated but charming larger-than-life actor Richard Burton. He was loud and rowdy, but those famous eyes gave him license. He had voluminous presence.

René was welcoming us with hugs and kisses while his wife, Mary, stood by waiting to hand us menus.

"They don't need menus," René announced with a dismissal of his hand. "I will cook for them myself."

He held my mother's hand a little longer than he needed to, I think, and leaned in close to us. "Richard Burton is there; he's very happy this evening" he said, gesturing with his eyes. "Watch for the pretty one." He winked at me and left us.

We were excited by our nearness to the infamous actor, but anticipation at being cooked for by René was as enticing; René was a wizard. I believe that had he been young when the great chefs became public icons, he'd have eclipsed of Wolfgang Puck. We knew the mussels and lobster we came for would be the object of our desire, no matter who sat near us.

Mr. Burton entertained us with his roguish voice and exaggerated gestures. My mother sipped her martini specially made for her by Rocky, the bartender, who, like René, was dear to us. I believe I sipped ginger ale, though my mother may have ordered me a whiskey sour, as she sometimes did on special occasions. We laughed and joked like the good friends we were and reveled in the vibrancy of the busy restaurant. I was young and filled with dreams; it was an enchanting evening.

Twice since we arrived, Mr. Burton spilled his drink. He was served an enormous lobster; enshrined in a bib, his animation increased.

"My dears," he announced to the room, "this lobster is as divine as a virgin!" He then allowed his eyes to scan his audience, and seeing my flowering youth, promptly extended a sticky hand to me.

"Ah, my sweet, virginal flower, I am sorry if I embarrassed you, but this lobster has captured my senses." With that he turned back to his task of devouring what looked to be at least a two-pound lobster, and left us to our steaming pile of black mussels.

René, gracious host that he was, sat with us before or after we ate, sometimes both. He slid next to my mother and picked up a mussel, slurping it into his mouth.

"So sweet and hot," he said as he winked at my beautiful mother.

I doubt my mother realized her allure, not just in those days, either. My husband paid her a great compliment when we first dated: He said, "They say you can tell how a woman will look by her mother. I'm in good shape, then." What a charmer!

We enjoyed our mussels so much that if I close my eyes, I can taste the garlic broth and pieces of shallots floating among the black shells of each tender, juicy bite. What a privilege to have been entrusted with the recipe.

"Milk—that's the secret," René told my mother. But it was not until years later, when my friend Liz and I did him a favor and worked a Saturday night in the fall of 1980, that I actually saw him prepare those delicate little beauties. Shellfish is sexy eating— aphrodisiacs for sure.

We washed our hands with hot towels and munched on Caesar Salads, while Mr. Burton began singing *Somewhere in the Night*." His voice bellowed through the restaurant. Some diners were offended by his vociferous meandering, but we were charmed. After all, he was Richard the Great. It saddens me that the youth of today has no idea who he was.

I excused myself to the restroom. Exiting the ladies' room, I was faced with a wall of framed mirror. It beckoned every woman withdrawing from the door labeled Dames. As I was checking my look, a very unsteady Richard rounded the corner and stared at me. I blushed from my blonde head to the bottoms of my sandal-clad feet, feeling naked.

"You are lovely," he crooned.

Immobile, I stood smiling, my knees weak; even with traces of food on his chin, he was audacious. He extended his arm, escorted me to my table, and bowed deeply, reaching for my mother's hand, which he kissed.

When I sat down, he leaned across the black leather booth and said, "The lobster is as divine as you lovely ladies." We smiled, anticipating our crustaceans, but he continued to speak. "What are you celebrating?"

"My daughters sixteenth birthday," my mother answered, taken with his presence.

"Ah," he said, "a tender age." With that, he stood and left the restaurant.

I remember being so saddened by his death. Years later, when I saw Elizabeth Taylor in an airport, I wanted to say, "I would have married him twice, too." Who could mark their sixteenth birthday better than dinner with Lucia and Richard Burton, except to have been in the presence of "The King"—Elvis—which I was for my thirteenth birthday!

≈

René's Lobster

2 1–to-2 pound live Maine lobsters

2 glasses white wine (12 ounces, at least)

Diced shallots and garlic

Dash salt

Dash sugar

Fill a deep pot with salted and sugared water. Add shallots and garlic, and cook to a full and robust boil. (I add the 2 glasses of wine to the water in hopes that the lobsters get a buzz first.) When the water boils, speak to the lobsters gently, thank them, and drop them head-first into the boiling water. (My husband kills them first with a poker to the head; I just can't.) Boil until shells become red (approximately 10-12 minutes, depending on their size). Remove, rinse, and split with a large knife or cleaver. Cut down the middle, and rinse off any greenish or yellow gunk. If you are lucky enough to have a female with eggs, remove the red (orange-colored) roe, and add butter and lemon to it before devouring. (That is my favorite part.) Tie a dishtowel around your neck, and mangia!

LAYER 4

Father-Daughter Meatloaf

"It is easier for a father to have children than for children to have
a father."

John XXIII

In January of '77, I visited my father in Florida, thanks to a ticket he had sent me for Christmas. I was in California, having driven cross-country with my mother and two friends, but I hadn't been able to find a job as a waitress because I wasn't twenty-one, and I was unhappy being a cashier at Norm's. While riding the bus to the bank, someone cut my purse, which was draped across my shoulders, leaving me with only straps and without the $200 I worked so hard to save.

I stood at the bus stop in the rain, waiting for my uncle to pick me up when a motorcycle skidded on some oil and ran over my foot, breaking three of my toes! The motorcycle guy, draped in a Mexican poncho, shrugged his shoulders, flicked his cigarette butt at me, and drove away. I called the police; I had written down the license plate. They showed up forty minutes later, took my statement, and left me standing with swollen toes, a broken shoe, and purse straps. I was hard pressed for a reason to stay in the "Wild West." I floundered, ill at ease, homesick, and bored to tears.

I drove to Las Vegas with my aunt and grandmother. The plan was that we would see Frank Sinatra at Caesers Palace, then I would fly to Florida to hang out with Dad. My grandmother was in her late 60s then, a die-hard fan of Sinatra and a wicked gambler on the nickel slot machines. When I went looking for her before I left, her hands were black up to her elbows from playing those machines. Until she was 70, she rode the bus to Las Vegas to see her beloved and gamble all her coins. I will never forget her swooning over Frank singing "That's why the Lady is a Tramp."

I ran into a friend there who invited me to gamble with him and then see a burlesque show. It was exciting playing craps, he had a lot of cash on him and was handing me $100 bills. I was winning for a while, and the dealer began referring to me as "The Lady in Red." By 4 a.m., I was exhausted and eager to leave. He invited me to see a "burlesque" show: a twisted name for a girl who could shove hard boiled eggs inside of her and shoot them across the room. It was a far cry from Gypsy Rose Lee, and I was horrified!

This visit to Florida would be the only time I spent alone with my father before he disappeared. He was without his girlfriend at the time, and it was an opportunity I didn't want to pass up. I remind myself not to put time off with my loved ones; you just never know.

My plane landed in the afternoon, giving us the rest of the day to get acquainted. I strode out of the air-conditioned terminal into the humid arms of Fort Lauderdale. I saw his car parked in the loading zone. The sun danced off his blonde highlights as it trickled through the sunroof. He smiled, blue eyes framed with long, straight, blonde lashes partially hidden by ridiculously small silver-rimmed sunglasses.

He stepped out of the car to help with my luggage, then he asked, "Can you cook like your mother?"

Determined to reach this place of esteem she still held with him, I replied, "Better."

"Let's see," he smiled from the corner of his mouth, his cigar clenched between his teeth. We drove to the market, both of us singing to Frank Sinatra on the 8-track cassette player. We are all Frank Sinatra fans.

We went to Publix because my father didn't like the Piggly Wiggly store. This was not the first time I'd food shopped with him. Once, my brother and I took off from school in the winter to drive to Florida with Daddy. We went with him to the market because we always bought the food when we stayed with my Aunt Bella in West Palm Beach. He spent $100 and filled two carts! At the time, that was extravagant!

The market was crowded with small, white- and blue-haired people who never said excuse me or moved their carts to the side so we could pass them. We were used to waiting on this kind of clientele in New York, but they sure could be rude. I was smiling because for the first time in a long, long time, I was holding my father's hand. It was brief, but it was heaven.

≈

Meatloaf

Ingredients:

1 pound lean, chopped ground beef

1 egg

1 cup breadcrumbs

2 cloves garlic

Salt

Oyster sauce or beef base (paste)

1 tablespoon finely chopped onion (optional)

Ground black pepper

1 tablespoon olive oil

Fresh Italian parsley

I placed the ingredients in our cart, acutely aware of my father's casual scrutiny. I was selecting for our first and only meal alone since grammar school; when he picked me up early for a dental appointment. After, he took me to Burger King for a Whopper; my lip was still numb and I bit a hole in it. I didn't care, because I was alone with him. I savored every moment of our day and night together; history had shown me that these times were fleeting. I was correct in my assumption; the next day he went on a blind date. She stole him from me until Umus, the mother of my stepbrother, arrived from New York, eclipsing our eventuation.

Once, when we were sitting on the beach watching his son play in the sand, my father said, "I know I messed up with you kids and Mommy, and I want to do better this time. I know you understand."

I said I did, and I was crazy about that baby. But, really, I was jealous, and I didn't understand why he wouldn't try harder with us too; after all, we, his first children, were only teenagers.

When Umus arrived, she took over. At first, I wasn't thrilled, but figured I would try for some normalcy with him and his new family; it had been a very long time since I'd experienced a two-parent household. I was learning about acceptance. Umus was great at first, but little by little, I felt as though she wanted me to go and that she wanted the family she created with my father to be the focal point of his life. They were never married, though, so I wonder how much he really loved her.

In the market, I picked out White Rose potatoes, spinach, and Romaine lettuce. My father added wine, vodka, vermouth, beer, and hard salami. We separated to make our selections, reuniting at our cart; it was a magical dance of familiar strangers. I don't ever remember feeling so connected to him. We drove home with nine paper bags neatly nestled in the trunk of his silver Mark IV; it had maroon corduroy upholstery—really. Sun and salt air caressed our faces through the open sunroof while Sinatra crooned "*Some Enchanted Evening.*"

I watched Hallandale become Hollywood Beach as we crossed the bridge. The Atlantic Ocean highlighted the sandy coast as we drove north toward my father's house on North Surf Road. I swallowed every detail of the passage, savoring it like a vintage wine; I can almost taste the salty air as I write this.

We parked in front of the house I thought I'd someday inherit. It was connected to five other units then owned by an eccentric, retired movie star, Joan Fontaine, who was a relic and a real character. Her voice was a combination of an aged Bette Davis and Mrs. Howell (on *Gilligan's Island*). When he took possession of the unit in the early '70s, Ms. Fontaine was charmed by my father. I'm certain his women distressed her, as their youth was a reminder of the loss of her own.

During one of my visits, I was left with Teresa, my father's twenty-two-year-old girlfriend. I was sixteen at the time. In a way, my dad had abandoned us both, so we made the most of our time together. She was a dangerous, troubled young woman; I had to be careful with the secrets I trusted her with. But she was close enough to my age, and on the young side in her behavior, so we did have some fun.

One evening, Teresa and I were invited to dine with Joan; she was quite inebriated when she extended a dinner invitation to the two of us. It was her intention, I believe, to befriend Teresa and me so she could manipulate my father to her will. I don't think he ever paid her the balance of the money he owed her for the balance of her condo purchase. Poor Joan, thinking we could help; silly woman.

Her apartment was the largest of all the units. It was located on top of the five lower units. It was filled with antiques and movie paraphernalia from her past. Her bed was centered in the middle of the large quasi-loft. It sat high off the ground with giant tufts of white pillows and down coverlets. The floors were turquoise tile with animal-skin rugs scattered over them. A wraparound porch afforded her a view that overlooked the Atlantic Ocean, a magnificent palate of turquoises and blues. Although it had tacky elements, it was eclectic and filled with wonderful photos of earlier period stars and largely framed snapshots of her.

In her youth, she was a beautiful Marilyn Monroe-type blonde, full bodied with voluptuous, red lips. It was fascinating for me—and sad. She had not aged well, reminding me of Bette Davis in the movie *"What Ever Happened to Baby Jane?"* She spoke in a shrill, singsong tone laced with vodka and some kind of pills she kept in her silk kimono pocket.

She made us martinis straight up, followed by raw ground beef, which she called steak tartar. I poured my drink in a plant, and when she wasn't looking, we lobbed our tartar out the window. The next day, after a run on the beach, I smelled meat cooking. I could see there was no one barbequing, so I went to investigate the smell. I found the tartar browning in the hot sun on the hood of Joan's powder-blue Cadillac!

I drove Ms. Fontaine to many errands. I felt a compassion for her; she was lonely and alone. Eventually, however, her treatment of me became reproachful as her relationship with my father deteriorated; she chose not to pay me. I took another job waiting on tables, leaving her with no replacement. I felt sorry for her, though I don't know why exactly. It appeared to me she had already died inside, which is hard to ignore.

We carried the packages inside; I changed into shorts while my father opened up the house. The sea was slightly rough; a breeze was blowing into our living room. My father settled himself on the sofa in front of the screen doors facing the ocean. He opened the paper and summoned me to make him a martini—as much a test as the dinner I would prepare him. I knew I had him here, though; I'd watched my mother make them a million times. I took out the shaker glass from the freezer, added ice, poured a little vermouth in, and swirled it around. I cored a lemon, rubbed the peel around the edge of the chilled martini glass, and poured out the vermouth. I then added the Smirnoff vodka and walked it over to my father.

"Thank you, Daughter," he said, motioning to me to put it on the waiting coaster.

His eyes never left the newspaper, though I felt them on me just the same. He looked studious in a nerdy way, sporting reading glasses that were also too small for his face.

I walked into the kitchen and switched on the radio kept on the windowsill. I pulled out a metal bowl and a casserole dish and preheated the oven to 375 degrees. I washed my hands and opened the package of sirloin, which the butcher had ground for me. There is something very comforting about the white paper it came wrapped in; it reminded me of a freshly diapered baby.

I put the meat in the bowl and added the breadcrumbs and eggs. I always mix these ingredients first to give the meat a chance to soak up the eggs and crumbs; otherwise, you can end up with dry meatloaf. I chopped the onion finely, and poured myself a glass of wine. I felt nervous for some reason and wanted to look like a pro. I finely chopped the garlic to add to the sautéed onions with olive oil and a little salt. Here's a tip: Heat onions and garlic only enough to marry the ingredients.

I chopped the parsley while grooving and Curisin' with Marvin Gaye on the radio, feeling the warm effects from my two sips of wine. My father finished his martini and stood on our seawall, talking to our neighbor, Bill. I dropped the parsley and onions on top of the meat then added the salt, pepper, and a good dollop of oyster sauce. With my hands, I kneaded these ingredients together, letting them marinate while I peeled the potatoes and put them in salted water to boil. It's a rule in our family; meatloaf goes with mashed potatoes and gravy. While the water came to a boil, I molded the meat into the casserole dish (or you can use a baking pan) and painted the top of the loaf with the remaining oil in the sauté pan.

Decrease oven temperature to 350 degrees. Meatloaf takes about 25 minutes, depending on the servings and oven.

*** TIP: Using leaner meat and adding olive oil rather than fatty meat makes a huge difference in flavor.

I washed the spinach while my father washed the seawall and hosed down the beach chairs. He liked to water and sweep; it's relaxing—good for thinking and mindless wandering, he said. I agree and still do both, especially when I am anxious or upset.

Fresh spinach shrinks up when it is cooked, so use the whole bunch. Pinch off the ends to avoid toughness. Place a saucepan filled with salted water on the burner; drop the spinach in when it boils, but only long enough for it to wilt. Then drain and pat it dry. Put a little more olive oil in the frying pan. Add more chopped onion and garlic with pinches of salt and pepper, and stir it over a low heat for about 5 minutes; then cover and let it sit for a while.

While the potatoes and meatloaf were cooking, I set the counter. My father was in the midst of redecorating and had no table; the counter seemed more intimate, anyway. I used the dishes that were in the cabinet and wondered where they came from. I set a brown and gold dinner plate, a salad plate, a folded paper towel, and silverware in front of each of our stools. I recognized the glasses as those from Oceans III, a restaurant our family had owned on the beach in Westhampton. I remembered the dishes were from another restaurant, The Swiss Chalet. I put out two wine glasses, glasses of water, and the bottle of wine. I didn't like wine then. I just tolerated it like other grown-up things, but since I was a bit anxious, I had a second glass.

"Daddy, dinner," I called out. He turned toward the screen door as though he could see me, but I knew he could not.

"It smells good, Daughter," he said while walking toward me. I smiled and motioned for him to sit down while I took out the meatloaf. I dumped butter, milk, salt and pepper, and a small amount of sour cream into the potatoes and furiously mashed them while he washed his hands. The meatloaf had made a nice amount of drippings, and I was able to make good, quick gravy.

Good, Quick Gravy

With a paper towel, remove any of the excess floating grease or sediments from the pan. Turn the burners on low. (The baking dish can go right on the burners at a very low heat.) Sprinkle flour into the pan, and beat with a fork or, preferably, a whisk. I use Wondra flour because it is very light, but regular flour will do.

***TIP: If you do not have flour, you can use cornstarch. But it's trickier because it thickens very quickly, so you need to put a small amount of gravy into a separate dish and add the cornstarch while whisking it to get the lumps out.

When the remaining gravy begins to boil, add to the mixture and whisk constantly. Add a combination of water and wine to the gravy. Sprinkle flour until it maintains the right consistency and good flavor, then sprinkle salt and pepper to taste. Serve immediately.

While I was finishing the gravy, my father took his fork and dug a hole in the middle of the meatloaf. He smiled and made a sound that told me he approved, and then he sat down and waited for me to serve him. My father demanded to be served—a habit I still employ with my own family of men.

Once all the courses were put on the table, I tossed some lettuce with olive oil and vinegar and sprinkled it with a little garlic salt and fresh ground pepper, then squeezed a little lemon on it.

"Salute," my father said, touching his glass to mine; we ate. I don't remember the conversation from that meal, or if we spoke at all. I know it was a success. Later, while we were walking on the boardwalk, my father commented, "You're like her, but your mother is the best cook. She'll always be Lucy Legs, the best cook, to me"

LAYER 5

Tea on the Veranda

"Train up a child in the way he should go: and when he is old, he will not depart from it."

Proverbs 22:6

Everyone has impacted and shaped my life since I was a young girl—some good, some not so good. Our neighbors when we lived on South Road, for example, Bill and Helen Denkowitz, a retired couple, were dedicated to the beautification of their home. I went over there often to learn and help. Helen taught me many tips that I rely on still—for example, how to germinate marigolds, store them in a shoe box and plant them the next year. I also learned if you plant marigolds as a border, the rabbits won't eat your tomato plants.

Helen and Bill had lovely gardens filled with flowers and vegetables. They were a nice, older couple, and they took me under their wing when I was alone because my parents were at work.

When you grow up on the East Coast, seasons benchmark renewal and cessation. I still change my slipcovers and put my white clothes away, and though the weather stays hot, my inclination is to unpack my sweaters as soon as Labor Day is over. Last year it was decided by the fashion gurus that white could be worn all year, and not just winter white. It just doesn't feel right to me. I have grown to appreciate the less subtle seasonal changes of the West, but each May, I hunger for walks down Lilac Lane, lined with a riot of purple delicacies—a sensory memory that still makes my nostrils twitch with bliss.

Kay Carre was a woman versed in the old school of etiquette. She was married twice; both husbands died, leaving her comfortably set, yet I am certain, lonely. Kay was stately looking, like a president's wife. She had white hair and stern but warm eyes, framed with crinkles like Santa Claus. Her long face had an aristocratic look to it; you could sense she had good breeding. She wore clothes from Lilly Pulitzer and Talbot's, and always had shoes and a bag to match. She was not affectionate but possessed certain "warmth" by her actions. Kay was my friend Kim's grandmother.

Kim and I have been lifelong friends. We had known each other briefly when we were children in the neighborhood of South

Road and Tanners Neck Lane. We renewed our acquaintance in the '70s when she returned home to Westhampton Beach after attending Whittier College in California.

Her family lived in a white stucco house with Spanish-style landscaping. The previous owners planted some vegetation foreign to our soil—a plant commonly called gypsum weed. With trumpet-like blooms, the plant's seeds contained poisonous belladonna alkaloids that I ingested and almost died from; I was tricked by Paul Sparrow-a kid in the neighborhood I liked, said they were the white seeds from a watermelon and that they had all eaten them. The seeds inside the pods of the plant taste sweet and are hallucinogenic. I never tried LSD because, technically, I tripped in the third grade. Kim's family had moved out before my episode with the hallucinogenics.

In elementary school, Kim was a freckled-faced girl with thick, blonde hair falling down her back. Her green eyes were always shy but smiling. I was jealous; she was picked for team sports in the neighborhood since she was fast and coordinated, and she already had large breasts. With my blonde hair and green eyes and despite my Italian blood, Kim and I were often taken for sisters, much to our delight and wishful thinking.

When Kim was around eleven, her mother, who had been ill, was taken in the middle of the night—literally. Kim's mother was a beautiful young woman afflicted with polio early in her life. Kim and her brothers were confined to a bedroom, leaving them to guess and agonize about their mother's condition. Kim peeked out to catch a glimpse of her mother being taken away on a stretcher. It was a chaotic incident.

For three days, Kim and her brothers huddled together in fear with no idea their mother had died. It wasn't until Kim overheard them speaking of funeral arrangements that she learned her mother had died of an aneurysm. No one held Kim, gently stroked her lovely hair, or comforted her with the words "It's okay, Sweetie. Your mommy is with the angels." Instead, she and her two brothers were shuffled around until their future could be determined.

Eventually, a grieving Kay took Kim and her brothers to her home. Kim's father was in a terrible state; he was a heavy drinker and loved her mother deeply. I suppose because adults thought it was better to shelter the children, no one thought to explain the details until Kim asked direct questions. My heart is heavy as I recall this story that I pulled from Kim's heart and memory many years later. Though I understand the times were different, and today it seems kids get way more information than is necessary, Kim must have died inside, unable to say her goodbyes, to grieve properly, and to have her daddy to fall back on.

Kay played a role in my life as well as Kim's, though it wasn't until I began recalling that time that I realized how important a role she played. Kay taught me how to prepare a tea party, a ritual, a celebration, a connection to a world I fantasized about.

My tea party knowledge was enhanced with my alliance to Kim. There are many people I hold dear because they exposed me to different types of teas and ways to drink them. Mrs. Terchun, our landlord and my friend Rosemary's mother, would tell me to put on a kettle for tea while the dryer tossed its contents and the washer swished and moaned. On those cold winter days when we shared the laundry room, I explored cups of steaming herb teas, and Mrs. T's wisdom. On one occasion, Mrs. Terchun drove Rosemary and me to Riverhead, where I enjoyed my first professional manicure.

"You have lovely hands," Mrs. T complimented me, "and nicely shaped nails." I recalled her compliments later in my life when I felt unattractive; it always lifted my spirits.

Of course, my first introduction to tea was at home. My mother gave me tea with lemon and honey for a cold and tea with milk for a stomachache. Tea has been comforting me, I think, because it was given to me by women who loved me.

Sipping tea has remained a source of pleasure—a vehicle for social activities and an invitation for savory talk long overdue. Tea is for hunkering with a book in front of a fire or for extended locution or parlance; it's a medium for neutrality. Tea is universal; it is its own language. Fortunetellers have long thought that there is information in the tea leaves stranded at the bottom of a cup. Tea is a confidant—a holder of secrets and promises. It is a magical elixir inherited from our past. I remain a tea aficionado;-totaler, each cup connects me to the past.

When Kim returned to Long Island in the '70s, we began dancing in clubs after work. We closed many a discotheque. I remember well and have longed for one night at Scarlet's when we worried over nothing more than our wardrobe and if John (one of the owners) would let us in without paying the cover charge.

Like Kim, Kay was interesting, and I wanted her to like me. Kay's sense of the proper etiquette gave me the opportunity to exercise my knowledge from my two years at Barbizon modeling school. Kay and Kim were uniquely conflicting in their personalities and characters. Where Kay was elegant, Kim was sexy. Where Kay was conservative, Kim was adventurous. Where Kay was concerned, Kim was aloof. There was a time I idolized Kim; her beauty and ability to draw people to her made her sexy and alluring. Conversely, Kay enchanted me with her poise and self-assuredness. They never appeared to need to fit in. Although they were a contrasting pair, they carried themselves confidently.

One of my greatest gifts is the ability to invite laughter. I am quick and witty, and the reward of laughter is candy for my soul. As children, my brother and I would make ourselves laugh until we cried. Truly, if you laugh hard enough, you will cry; if you cry hard enough, you will laugh. That's a good recipe, either way.

I made it my mission to break the ice when I was in the presence of Kim and Kay; making them laugh was a priority, and I was successful at it. I still save up stories and jokes to get Kim laughing. Before she laughs, she gets a look on her face as if she's uncertain your comedic act will warrant laughter, then she lets it go, and I am undone. To be allowed to know Kim is a gift. I have a collection of friends;, each holds a place of honor, each cherished. I was fortunate to add Kim to the band of women I call my sisters.

Though I admired Kim's separate reality as the author of her own rules, I saw how those rules alienated her. Kim, whose aloof nature had a tendency to keep people at a distance, became a challenge to me. That probably sounds weird, but I am like that. If someone does not like me, well, that's okay. I just want to know why—no, I needed to know why.

Let me clarify that statement; I have outgrown that need. Curiosity gets to me at times, but I have so many wonderful people to give myself to and be received by, willingly, that I barely spend time on those who take lots of work or make me crazy.

Crazymakers were once my fascination. I was drawn to them like a bee to honey; I had almost a sick obsession. One day, I realized the reason was by focusing all my time and energy on them, I could put off taking care of myself, which was painful, frustrating, and scary. I don't dislike them; now, I sense them, say a silent release prayer, and move on. I have much more time to invest in myself and those who give back to me.

Kim's rules, just as Kay's boundaries for Kim, forged a wedge between them. I rode shotgun for both of them—a curious position of observation. I was born a mother and took my vocation seriously. In retrospect, I needed to be Kay's granddaughter and Kim's mother. There must be something Freudian there. Eventually, Kay and Kim filled some of each other's gaps, but the lightheartedness was often vacant. Kay was not a carefree person, and Kim had a tendency to withdraw into her little world of angst.

When I became a mommy, I saw the shortcomings of my parents. At first, I said what everyone else said: "Well, they did their best." Their imperfections, their tendencies to focus on their young lives, dropping us anywhere so they could work or play, and their dramas seemed a right of passage after the suffering they'd each experienced. I turned tolerance into love. It was my ratio: Acceptance equals them still loving me.

I have heard it said that you do not truly become a parent until your own parent dies. When I lost my father, I realized how much of a child I was; I saw his youth as well. Eventually, children become parents to their parents. It seems a natural order—the ebb and flow, the give and take of life. It was certainly the case for Kim and Kay.

As Kay, aged Kim became her cornerstone. They deepened their love for each other, and though they differed in opinions about the life-style Kim led, inside, Kim was a lot like Kay, and the young girl in Kay lived vicariously through Kim. Kay disapproved of many of Kim's activities, especially staying out late. However, in some of her own youthful memories she cherished-her tolerance grew.

I met Kay in the summer of 1978 when Kim and I drove her olive-green Fiat from Ft. Lauderdale, Florida, to Long Island, New York. It was a great road trip, in spite of the Fiat's nature to break down. One mechanic declared that the letters FIAT stood for "Fix it again, Tom." He was not far from wrong. But it got us to Kay's house intact.

Kay lived in a spacious home on Aspatuck Lane in Westhampton Beach. Her shiny, wood floors reeked of money and good taste. The walls were white and clean looking with good pieces of art and slipcovers that changed with the seasons. It was a place that kept me rooted, and I felt safe there during a time in my life when I had no guidance. It was the tail end of the '70s; drugs were common, recreation was the desired career, and the restaurant business was a perfect way to start the day penniless and end it buying champagne. We were a fearless, misdirected generation raised by divorced parents, who were cheating or repressed and comfortable indulging their children with freedoms they had been denied.

I had friends who had more structured family lives, and I had a place with them as well. I lived at Geraldine's house all through high school, and I am a balanced person because of it. Kate Sweet, Geraldine's mother, was widowed too soon. She raised five children alone, and I became her sixth. I was nomadic after my parents divorced, and Mrs. Sweet welcomed me, guided me, and reprimanded me when I needed it. She stocked her kitchen with healthy foods and kept Nestle's Strawberry Quick for my milk. Because these women took me in, I felt like I was privy to the tendrils—the family ties I was ravenous for while my own family searched for an anchor. I hungered for security, a normal family life, and two parents who loved each other and us.

It took many years and therapy to release my need for flight; with no ties to family or community, I felt safer moving from place to place. My father called me the "Gypsy"—the pot calling the kettle black, I think.

Kay was horrified with our lifestyle, and now I see why. We were reckless in our abandon, as youth often are; assured in our ignorance that we knew what was good for us. I have revisited my childhood longingly in search of the simplicity and safety I enjoyed before our family was perforated. I ache sometimes for the one drive I remember when the four of us sang in the car on the way to my Aunt Hope's for Christmas Eve. I create and hold rituals of togetherness in my own family in hopes that a chasm will never separate us as it did my first family, so our children will be the benefactors of the heirloom rituals we have built for them.

I searched for roots during much of my life; I am hungry for the memories of the elderly—the lineage of wisdom that is waiting to be presented by these aged bodies whose spirit lingered beyond their youth. I suppose due to my need for connection, I befriended antiquated people when I was young, often preferring their company over someone my age because I was hungry for the sentinel of their memories.

I retain details from these wise natives of days gone by and the ones I enjoy at present. Some have taught me lessons in gardening and cooking; others, in living and dying. I enjoy the company of my own grandmother now that we live on the same coast. She lacks the elegance and etiquette Kay possessed, but she has a genuine zest for life; at 88 she survived a double-valve replacement and is still pretty independent. I pray I am heir to her energy, her independence, and her desire to keep moving. She is quite a character.

In those days, my grandmother lived in California, and I had no relationship with her. She was busy raising my aunt, who came to her late in life; she is a year younger than me. I kept in touch with my Titas (our word for aunt), who lived up the island from us in Huntington. But they were busy with their own lives and children. So to have Kay was paramount to my continued development. The role of each generation in a person's growth creates the layers needed to form each level. Without Kay, I would have missed a cherished material used to build my foundation. I have a notion that those without any older generations in their lives miss a key element to fully understand the cycle of life.

I was sorry to move West. I love Long Island. I thought I'd marry and raise my children there; they would attend the same schools, swim in the same ocean, and my friends' children and my own children would be friends.

I missed Kay as much as my friends at times. I relished our friendship and kept in touch as often as I could. I lost the enhancements of her lifestyle when I left. Because my upbringing differed from Kim's dramatically, I was delighted to be exposed to Kay's modeled social graces and influences. Kim had been bred to go to good schools, marry the right people, and belong to a country club. My parents were interested in my breeding, but even the Barbizon School of Modeling, where I was versed in poise, etiquette, and fashion, was not the same as learning how to steep tea and make finger foods from a woman with Kay's training.

I credit my parents for their efforts and determination to educate me in manners and breeding. As restaurant/bar business owners, we were not considered tailored in the world of socialites; perhaps it was the British ancestry of our peers we lacked. Our ancestors came over on boats with names belonging to olive oil and imported delicacies. With locals, we could hold our own; eventually we became natives. Using diplomacy, respecting our elders, saying please, thank you, and things of that nature were drilled into my psyche.

My parents were big on respect, something I truly honor them for. Many of the kids of the upper class we waited on had no manners at all; I attribute that to a false sense of heightened placement. Respect was drummed into our heads; certainly, if felt undeserved much of the time.

"You don't have to like them," my mother would say, "but by virtue of their years on this earth, they have earned reverence."

I believe because of these cultured courtesies, I am comfortable in all settings, and as a kid, I was welcome in all my friends' homes. I gained insight into the world of adults, and Kay allowed me into hers. I felt special, because it seemed to me that Kay liked and approved of me.

Though Kim's and my journey began as one of tutelage, we eventually became women entrenched in life. Kay invested love, money, and effort into Kim's place in the world; my own future had potential, but the backing was not really there. My father dropped out of school, and my mother got pregnant fairly young. Neither of my parent's childhood homes fostered the etiquettes I was interested in. Being in Kay's home gave me a "hands-on" education; certain behaviors were expected. I repaid her with respect and eagerness to learn her skills in homemaking.

In retrospect, I see the true impact this woman had on my perceptions. In my own home, I have created a warm, welcoming version of Kay's beautiful home; save for the revolving door of kids.

Kay's home sat higher than the driveway, the style of many builders then. A formal country-style home with a comfortable sunroom, it was filled with beautiful antiques, china, and crystal. My visits to Kay's were unforgettable, and I cherished them. I had little opportunity to be around such beautiful things, and was invited to use them for eating and drinking. Kay served us on china plates; we ate with sterling flatware and used linen napkins. Her home became a finishing school for me. I had a bed in Kim's room with crisp, expensive sheets. Today, lying on crisp cotton sheet takes me back to Kim's room on those coveted nights.

Kim was annoyed at Kay's interests in her life. She rebelled against her tutelage, feeling bossed and nagged. Though I

93

commiserated with her plight, secretly, I thought she was lucky to have someone who cared enough to look after her. My parents were deeply involved in their own lives. They loved me, cared about me, and tried to be available when I needed them, but they offered me no structure or boundaries. I had no one to be accountable to in the way Kay expected Kim to be to her. I viewed Kay's concern as love; Kim saw it as interference.

I understood. I think people of means feel entitled to certain rights, privileges, and control. Because Kay loved Kim as a daughter, she accepted me. She felt comfortable extending her opinions to me, allowing me some of the privileges and structures I hungered for. She chided us on our use of makeup and clothing. To me, this was the very thing I was lacking—someone to be accountable to—and I missed it with my mother living 3,000 miles away and when my father disappeared and I had to move.

Aside from "our" bedroom, my favorite room in her home was the veranda, or the sun porch, which was nestled in the rear of the house close to the woody area so prevalent on Long Island. There were windows on all sides where we could view deer, rabbits, and birds, all of which graced us with their presence on those lovely days with Kay.

"Tea on the veranda" became Kim and my favorite exclamation of high society. I coveted the finger foods, delicate salads, and tea served to us as we sat on overstuffed green and white cushions, pillowing out of white wicker furniture.

One exquisite spring day, minutes from summer, with Kay's wisteria adorning the sides of one wall, lavender-colored lilac bushes flooded us with scents of childhood. Kay was about to make the tea, when I asked if I could help while Kim took a shower.

"Of course; wash your hands. There is a proper way to prepare tea, Dear," she offered, "and it's high time you learned. When I was a girl, making tea was a lesson at school."

Studying her from my place at the sink, she winked, knowing she was about to divulge coveted wisdom. A delicate Wedgwood china teapot was removed from the cupboard and gently put in my hands. It was white with vines of pale, purple violets dripping down its sides. On the very tip of the lid, it had the tiniest violet bud—I can close my eyes and recall it exactly.

She instructed me to rinse the pot inside and out, pouring out the rinsing water.

"Always heat the pot so it doesn't crack from the boiled water," she said, and filled it with hot tap water.

Enjoying our interaction, she retrieved various supplies from the fridge and cupboards, placing everything on the counter in accordance with its use.

"Wash this watercress please, Dear," she said, handing me a bunch of greens that looked like fat clovers or some gangly weed from the garden.

I pulled off the band, separated the bunch, pinched off yellow ends, and rinsed them in the running water. She had a platter of other sandwiches, and I was supposed to emulate her work. I liked the small pieces of bread waiting to become sandwiches made for a baby's hands, and, of course, cultured young women.

Kay continued to arrange butter cookies on the violet vines that swept across her china, explaining the importance of good dishes to enhance the occasion. When the tea was opened, my nostrils twitched with the scent of orange, lemon, and a spice I think was cinnamon. She situated the loose, black tea leaves into a porcelain tea ball placed into the drained teapot and poured hot water over it. Instantly, the water bled—amber streamers swirling from the tiny holes of the tea ball, blending the water with its exotic ingredients. We placed silver, cups, saucers, napkins, and salad plates along with the teapot, honey, lemon, and assorted sandwiches on an oval, monogrammed, silver platter. Kay and I placed our fare on the glass covered wicker coffee table on the sun porch. She poured tea for Kim and me, and then for her, which was proper. She told me, "A lady serves herself last."

From that time, I mimicked Kay's every movement, allowing the experience to imprint my memory and my heart. This was my first tea party since I was a small child. Hot tea gave me a sense of safety and comfort. Perhaps it is drinking liquid amber, or merely the warm, smooth serum luxuriously sliding down my throat. Possibly it is the delight of using a teapot.

I love teapots. Once, when I was seven years old, I collected refundable bottles to redeem at Katrinka's, a deli store near our restaurant, to save up for a tea set. It was lovely, with a small vase for a single, petite blossom. The day I purchased that tea set, I carried it home on my bike, but slid on some gravel and fell to the ground along with my coveted tea set. I cried and cried. Conceivably that is the reason the ritual of the tea party—my first experience of a veranda and the warmth of a lovely older lady—embroidered a comforting memory I relish and partake in often.

≈

Recipes, Ingredients, and Rituals for a Tea Party

Watercress Sandwiches:

Miniature rye bread or rye crisp crackers

Butter, mayonnaise, or cream cheese

1 bunch watercress, washed and cleaned

Spread butter lightly over rye slice or cracker. Add watercress, at least two leaves on top of slice. Sprinkle with salt (optional).

Lettuce Cups

1 head of butter (Boston) or iceberg lettuce (your preference, as long as it will create a canoe-type of cup to hold other ingredients)

2 chicken breasts, cooked

1 cup washed red grapes (seedless and cut in half)

1 cup sliced almonds

1 cup finely chopped celery

1 tablespoon finely chopped scallions

1-3 tablespoons mayonnaise (Add it 1 tablespoon at a time; the mixture should be tacky, not gooey.)

½-1 teaspoon dill (to taste)

Small dash of coriander (Too much will overpower the salad.)

1-2 teaspoons lemon juice (to taste)

1-2 teaspoons lime juice (to taste)

I like to lightly pan sauté the breasts, but any style of cooking will work. My suggestion: Pour 2 to 3 tablespoons of olive oil into a deep frying pan. Sprinkle bottom of pan with breadcrumbs, lemon pepper, and garlic salt. Place breasts into pan—use medium-high heat—then sprinkle same ingredients on top of the breasts. Let cook until brown and lightly crusted; turn and repeat. Turn heat down once you get the scald on the chicken. Cool, and cut into chunk-sized slices.

Combine ingredients, adding mayonnaise a little at a time and lemon and lime juices last. Creating cup-like pieces with lettuce, stuff salad into lettuce. You should be able to hold this like a taco, so choose crisp lettuce with some body to it.

Petite Tomato Tuna Surprise

1 dozen cherry tomatoes (Any small tomato will work.)

1 can albacore tuna packed in water (Fresh tuna is delicious and easy to prepare hours before.)

1 pinch fresh dill, chopped fine

2 shallots, minced very small

1 teaspoon freshly ground ginger (optional)

2 dashes lemon pepper

2-3 tablespoons mayonnaise

1 teaspoon lemon (or to taste)

Fresh parsley

1 teaspoon capers

Cut tomatoes in half; gently scoop out seeds with small melon baller, and set aside. If using canned tuna, wash several times, and drain very well. If using fresh tuna, chose a firm, fresh piece of albacore tuna, preferably white meat. Wash fish, and pat dry with towel. Rub fresh dill on fish, and sprinkle lightly with pepper. Cook fish on a grill or in a broiler.

*** TIP: Spraying the grill with Pam prior to heating it or broiling pan if cooking in the oven will keep the fish from sticking. REMOVE GRILL BEFORE SPRAYING WITH PAM.

Cooking time of fish depends on thickness of filet—usually 6 minutes on each side check doneness by pushing on fish with finger—fish should rise up with juices bubbeling, but modify this accordingly. Remove fish and let cool, chilling for at least an hour before proceeding with recipe. Mash fish in a bowl, adding dill, shallots, ginger, lemon, and lemon pepper; mix well with fork.

Begin folding mayonnaise into mixture, tasting to assure you don't use too much, which can overpower the tuna. Mix tomato seeds into mixture, and then gently stuff them into tomato halves. Place on doily-covered platter or china dish; garnish with capers and parsley sprig.

This recipe can be used omitting mayonnaise completely, but I think just the right amount added is delightfully yummy.

Dainty Tea Brownies

2 squares milk chocolate (2 ounces)

⅓ cup butter

1 cup sugar

2 eggs

1 cup flour

1 teaspoon baking powder

1 teaspoon salt

Optional: 1 teaspoon mint extract (You can substitute crème de menthe—use twice the amount.)

Preheat oven to 350 degrees. Mix together flour, baking powder, and salt. In separate pan, melt together chocolate and butter in either a double boiler or microwave. Beat in sugar, eggs, and mint, then slowly add dry ingredients. Spread dough in 2 well-greased 13-by-9-inch oblong pans. (I use butter to grease the pans,) Optional: sprinkle with 1 cup finely sliced pistachio nuts. Bake 7-8 minutes; cut immediately into squares or diamonds. Remove from pan while warm.

*** TIP: The old method of melting butter is best because you have more control of the heat when melting the butter in a double boiler. To make your own double boiler, put one half to one cup of water into small saucepan and bring to boil. Using a Pyrex or metal measuring cup, melt butter and chocolate by placing the measuring cup into hot water; lower the flame. Melt slowly; stir often.

Ritual Recommendations

***TIP: 1. Invite one or more people, though I have thrown myself a "tea and me" party, and it worked out nicely.

***TIP: 2. Chose an elegant teapot, preferably china, ceramic, or glass. Stay away from metal; it can change the taste of the tea. Use your special teapot or borrow one; they are more durable then they look if handled correctly. Wash the teapot with warm, soapy water, rinse well, and dry it completely. Run the tap water on hot for a minute, and then fill up the teapot with hot water.

***TIP: 3. Fill a teakettle or a pot with water; bring to a boil.

***TIP: 4. Set a table somewhere cozy and inviting. If you don't have a veranda, use the space in front of a fireplace, window, or even under a painting; any warm setting will work nicely. Use your imagination; you could have your child draw you a picture, then include her or him in the ritual. Kids love tea parties! Or call your grandmother or your old Aunt Tilly. Someone has a teapot crying to be initiated into the ritual and is likely eager to join you! When my husband or my boys need TLC, I create this ritual for them, and they feel better.

***TIP: 5. Place cups and saucers, spoons, linen or pretty paper napkins, plates, cream, honey, sugar, lemon wedges, salads, finger sandwiches, cookies, or pastries on a table or some flat surface. When I was in my twenties, my roommate and I had no furniture. I went to a thrift store to barter for wooden crates.

The owner, Helene, offered me two crates, both missing one slat each, if I would dust her "knick-knacks." This took two hours, but it was worth it. We pushed the crates together and duct-taped them so the missing slats would be covered. Later, I walked to the fabric store and bought a remnant of Battenburg lace for $1.40. It fit nicely, and—voilà—we had a table. We used cushions discarded at someone's garage sale (we washed them first), and we had the perfect setting for my Oriental teapot given to me long ago by Geraldine.

***TIP:6. Create a mood; take the time to rejuvenate your lifestyle. Include such elegant rituals as a tea party; you deserve it. If you are a man and feel this type of tea party doesn't suit you, use your imagination; you might enjoy the ceremony and would certainly make an impression on your partner with the sentiment.

"It is not easy to find happiness in ourselves, and it is not possible to find it elsewhere," Agnes Replier wrote in *The Wisdom of Women.*

We need to treat ourselves in big and little ways, and you don't have to be rich to feel elegant like Kay or to make your life full. I will never forget Kay, her home, her love, and "tea on the veranda." As I lift my teacup in salutation, I honor the Kay in all of us. If you haven't found a Kay yet, look in a nursing home or call about elderly care. There are so many beautiful rituals and notions that need to be passed on by some sweet, older lady or gentleman; this is your gift waiting to be opened.

Kim and Kay remained close to each other for the rest of Kay's life. At times, it was challenging for Kim to listen and respect the ramblings of an old woman struggling to hold on to her life—as she knew it, it's not easy letting go. But in the end, they were two women loving, needing, and savoring one another's unique images.

Now that Kay is gone, Kim and I reflect on the many gifts Kay gave her—and us. She transitions through life as we all do, knowing, guessing, crawling, and standing tall. I believe her life is richer for the experiences she has survived. Her heart still beats through her many losses, and her soul, like mine, is nourished by the simple pleasures life affords us, like tea on the veranda. I honor that place from our youth by practicing that ritual at every age. I cherish those memories with Kay and mourn the loss of that youthful promise, but I revel in my life. It is rich and full because of special people and a promise that each cup of tea holds yet another ingredient to my own life's recipe.

LAYER 6

Bad Boy Brownies

"The Devil wrestles with God, and the field of battle is the human heart."

Fydor Dostoevsky

"Vengeance is mine sayeth the Lord."

I wonder if that means you ask God for help, and, suddenly, an idea forms in your head—or if it is the excuse we use for doing what we want and claiming, "God spoke to me." I'm sure it's somewhere in the middle.

In the case of "Luann vs. the Mean Boys of Barham," this idea just came to me—vindication for a cruel, hurtful act that left five young men hysterical with laughter and one young woman filled with shame.

I came cross-country in '76 with my mother's ex-boyfriend. I got the impression early on that he'd like to drive as far as New Jersey and stop, which was not my plan. He was in no rush; I couldn't wait to see what was next. At any rate, my mother had given me Black Beauties (diet pills) and Valium (relaxing pills) for the ride. Perhaps my mother had psychic abilities that she never organized into rational thought. We stopped for coffee and tea—my treat. I swallowed a "beauty" and dissolved a Valium in my ride's coffee. Sorry, buddy; I had a mission.

Life in the Hamptons in the winter can be really depressing if you are young, single and undirected. I was all three and hoped a trip to the West would offer this small-town girl some adventure—perhaps some answers. I suggested to my ride that, although the sky indicated the coming of evening, I was quite awake and ready to drive. So we watched the cities melt into a black blur as we sailed by in his convertible. The ride was comfortable, and he was okay with music we could both enjoy. With the awakening of light, his coffee kept him sleepy, and my tea kept me wide awake. We arrived in the City of Angels at dawn on the third day.

Los Angeles was an odd experience to behold. I remember a railroad track running directly down the widest expressway I'd ever seen. I thought, "This is not a road; it's an endless asphalt tongue, licking up cars by the dozens." The natives called it a freeway.

The amount of cars nudging each other for space conjured many thoughts, but "free" was not one of them.

Because I spent time in Florida, I was familiar with palm trees. However, these palm trees seemed thirsty, their long necks craning, twisting toward the sky in hopes of a drop of water. They were also barren, bearing no fruit. Later, I would know the skies of California hoarded their water so they could dump it all at once like an overfull awning. It seemed that nature had a special way of dealing with this quasi-desert state. It took many years for me to acclimate to the differences in the seasons.

Anyway, we headed toward an area that used to be called the Miracle Mile, somewhere around Wilshire Boulevard, A well-known concourse, it was my first destination in this foreign place. I slept on the sofa at my ride's friend's apartment. My memory is foggy because I was painfully anxious to make a connection with a friend or someone who would rescue me from my situation. Not that it was so bad; I was lonely and desperate for company my own age.

After several unanswered calls to my friend Riaz, who earlier in the summer had extended an invitation to me, I became depressed. I couldn't reach my aunt or my cousin, and I didn't want to stay with my grandmother, since I barely knew her, and she was older than the people I was with already.

What was I doing here? I yearned for a familiar face or some direct route other than the crusty liquor store—my only destination for more than a week. Finally, I was able to secure a ride to my aunt and cousin's house in the San Fernando Valley. The Valley was sad and disappointing to me, but at least there were people I knew. Everyone had lives, work, and schedules. I was homesick. I found work, though, and true to my nature, I put my best foot forward.

Through my mother, my father offered to send for me, but I was still aching from an experience with him that needed to heal. I wanted to prove to myself and to him that I could take care of myself, and I didn't need him. I stopped talking to my father for nearly two years, from age sixteen to eighteen. It was a dismal period. He disenchanted, hurt, and angered me so much that I tried to change my last name. My mother took my father's side. It was expensive to have my name changed legally and she wanted us to reconcile; after all, she had forgiven him for crimes close to the one he inflicted on me. I know she was angry with him for hurting me, and she wanted to exact physical pain on my grandfather. I was madder at my father; it was not her fault-she butted in to make peace.

I had fallen for my father's bull before, but I thought this time it would be different; he was usually pretty good with a promise. During spring recess he invited me to come to Florida. "We can spend some time together," he'd said. I thought he meant alone, just us; I was let down once again. He had a full house;—his awful family and a girlfriend, and little time for me. He invited my cousin, too; at least I had her.

I didn't mind being on my own there; he lived right on the beach, so I could easily amuse myself. It was so hot that the ocean lacked the enthusiasm to rush to the shore; it slunk slowly back like the eyelid of a sleepy child. It was boring; we had no car at our disposal and no money, and his parents wouldn't let us walk the boardwalk in the evenings. We reconciled ourselves to sitting at the kitchen counter after dinner playing cards—my father's youngest brother, his wife, my cousin, my grandfather, and myself. The air was so thick that it was hard to breathe. Even with every window open, it was stuffy and hot. We stayed in our bathing suits day and night.

The patriarch of the Puglisi family was an old diabetic, seriously lacking in hygiene, who liked Scotch and cheap cigars. The weather made him "nudgey." (Nudgey is a family word meaning a combination of anxious anticipation and edginess.) He walked around the condo looking for things to do. One night after the old man had had a few Scotches, his wife finally persuaded him to go to bed. He stumbled to the kitchen door, closing the glass challises in an attempt to lock up the house, I suppose.

I yawned and stretched in my sticky state of laziness.

"Oh, Grampa, it's so hot; please leave them open. I'll close them when I go to bed." I said this smiling sweetly at this man who had never liked me based on my blood relations to my mother, who he blamed for everything wrong in the world.

He moved quickly for an old man. So fast, in fact, I had no time to react as he flung himself at me, knocking me four feet to the ground; his hands grasped my throat while he shook me.

"You motherfucking cocksucker; you're just like your mother!" he said, exhaling a toxic combination of cigars and Scotch into my face.

His wife, Dorothy, screamed, holding her heart, "John, stop." She had a flair for drama, like the rest of us.

Everyone was screaming, trying to protect me, I thought. They finally pried him off me long enough for me and Annemarie, my cousin, to lock ourselves in my father's bedroom. My grandfather screamed obscenities and threw his old body against the door. I was scared and didn't understand what I had done to cause his outburst; even after the old bastard passed out, no one came to comfort me.

Annemarie was in the room with me, hysterical. I called my mother in New York for help. She was tending bar, and our friend, Chief of Police Doyle, was in for a cup of coffee when I called. He was calming and reassuring on the phone, promising that my father would take care of things when he came home. "Try to get some sleep, and keep the door locked," he'd recommended.

I slept tangled in my cousin's hair and tears until loud knocks and my father's angry voice boomed threats from the other side of the door. It was light out, around six in the morning. I could hear his mother crying to my father, "Sonny, my heart." Someone else said, "That little bitch, she just doesn't know when to stop." I still don't know who said that, or why. Stop what, I wondered? Annemarie and I stared at each other, speechless.

My father's voice assaulted me beyond the door: "Open the fucking door, Luann." It was surreal hearing him say my name. Usually, he called me "Daughter." He was ominous in his rage, and I shook with equal parts of fear and exasperation. I guessed any consolation he would have offered was to be reserved for his family; he listened to their lies, and I closed a door in my heart on them forever. I never referred to them as family again.

He continued to scream at the door; Teresa, his girlfriend—and I do mean girl—tried to persuade him to calm down. She tried to assure me it would be okay to open the door. I could tell his patience was running thin, and after a string of obscenities, something inside me snapped. My father's daughter jerked the door open with as much force as he had in trying to break it down. I stood in front of his hideous, red face, veins bulging and pulsating in his neck, his foul breath violating my nostrils with the putrid smells of liquor and cigars.

He was shuddering, staring at me as though I were an enemy. I was cringing inside, but I held his stare.

"You apologize to your grandfather, or your ass is going home," he said, spitting in my face just as his father had.

I moved past him and walked toward the room I shared with my cousins, grabbed my suitcase, and with him on my heels, shoved my belongings inside quickly. Briefly, I paused, looking straight

111

into his malevolent, blue eyes and said, "I should have known you would think it was my fault, him strangling me." He flew toward me with his hand ready to slap.

I held my ground, standing utterly motionless, and whispered, "Go ahead, hit me; I'll put your drunken ass in jail so fast you won't know what hit you." He stopped, his face expressing a myriad of emotions.

In retrospect, I believe he was crushed that I was not afraid of his threats, but some part of him was proud that I had the balls to stand up to his rage. I knew he didn't believe in hitting in the face or head, and I was beyond the belt and metal spatulas that had served him in the past. In that moment, I observed my father. Extracting every ounce of knowledge I'd gained of him, I used it against him; that is when I became his daughter, as though someone else lived inside me. He turned from me in disgust, and went to his room. "I'll deal with you in the morning."

He slept until two the next afternoon, had a few beers to calm his stomach and nerves, and drove us to the airport, stopping at Denny's because he was hung over and needed food. He had the nerve to lecture me and to tell me that until I apologized to everyone, I was not welcome there. I never said a word—just drank my tea and looked past him.

What a rotten bastard he was that day, and, somehow, I let my mother talk me into moving past that episode with him, making believe it never happened. But, it did happen, and as I sit writing this, I know I haven't forgiven him. I put it aside for the day when I could process my hurt and disappointment. I can't fathom a father who, seeing bruises on the neck of his ninety-pound, sixteen-year-old daughter, did not defend his child. What a coward. I lost complete respect for him.

With that memory still painful in my heart, I was in no hurry to go to Florida. Instead, I waited for something to happen in California. The wait felt eternal, but, finally, the phone rang, and it was for me.

When Riaz finally called, I thought things would be looking up. I drove with my aunt Patti, who is a year younger than I, to the apartment Riaz shared with some guys in Burbank on Barham Boulevard. They were a lively bunch of pot-smoking boys, mostly with no direction except for Mark, who seemed to have a goal. He was working at becoming an agent. He had a few comedians with gigs at various comedy clubs, and I was invited to join them to have some fun and experience the clubs in the area. I guess it was no secret that I developed a crush on Mark. He seemed to share my interests.

After some time, the holiday months were upon us, and lots of flirting took place. One night, we ended up alone in the bedroom he shared with Riaz. Things were heating up, and he began loosening some of my garments, when I heard a noise coming from the closet. Mark tried to distract me, but my senses kicked in, and I walked to the closet and opened the door. There was Riaz and the rest of the roommates, crammed into the closet trying to record Mark and me. I was horrified, embarrassed, and filled with shame. I grabbed my things and ran out the door. They fell all over themselves, laughing. No one even came after me—not even Mark. I heard only a voice—I think was Riaz's—saying it was only a joke.

I fogged up the windows with my clamoring, my body jolting in frustration. But after a few minutes with the cold, night air on my face, my father's daughter emerged. I can't reiterate how many times my father's daughter has saved my life, usurping power from the feeble victim I could become. I drove to Van Nuys down familiar streets newly wet with rain, and the idea came to me. I was tired of being the "sweet" girl everyone could depend on, or shit on, or hurt and rely on for forgiveness. I hated being a victim. I felt disappointed at my own pathetic desire for acceptance from even those losers.

Mostly, though, I was pissed. I sniffed hard and swallowed my innocence. From that moment on, I was possessed.

I steered the car into the parking lot of Lucky's market. I followed my footsteps down the aisles, stopping to gather ingredients I sought. I drove home hearing Rod Stewart sing *Maggie May* on the AM radio we kept in the car. Once back at my cousin's, I pulled my suitcase out. I decided to take my father's ticket and go to Florida before I went home to New York to find a job. I figured I could use his guilt to make myself feel better. That never works for me; it actually makes me feel worse, and I become sappy again.

I walked from my cousin's home, where she lived with her son, through the back yard and into the big house that belonged to my aunt and uncle. I went straight into the kitchen and turned on the oven. Uncle Vince came in from the bar and asked what I was doing.

"I'm making brownies for some friends," I said sweetly, because Vince was a good guy, and sometimes I told him my troubles.

"You're too nice to those boys," he said leaving me to my task.

I pulled out the ingredients I would need for my creation and answered him: "Uncle Vince, you have no idea!"

≈

Bad Boy Brownies

Ingredients:

1 box brownie mix (fudge packet included)

2 eggs (as per directions)

Water

Oil

2 large boxes of chocolate Ex-Lax

With the same flair as Betty Crocker, I mixed the ingredients in a bowl, licking the spoon one last time before I put the Ex-Lax in. I had ground the squares into powder so it would blend evenly into the mixture. Then I poured the Ex-Lax into the batter, put it in a greased baking dish, set the timer, and continued packing. The next day I dressed and had my cousin, Lori, drive me to Barham Boulevard. I enclosed the brownies with cellophane and put a note on the package that said, "I can take a joke. No hard feelings, Ha, Ha. LA." My heart pounded wildly in my chest; I feared they would hear it and open the door before I could ring the bell. I placed the brownies on the floor in front of the door. I took a deep breath and held it, put my finger to the doorbell, and pushed. I hid in the corridor down the hall to make sure they answered.

The door opened, and one of the guys picked up the brownies. He read the note and let out a hoot of laughter.

"Hey, come here; you won't believe it," he snickered out loud.

Two other roommates stepped out of the door, looking down the hallway. I ducked deeper into the alcove, still holding my breath, I think. Finally, the door closed, but before it did, I heard one of them say, "Desperate chicks; my favorite." Another one said, "Sucker."

I floated down the stairway. Lori had parked on the side of the building away from their window.

"What happened?" she asked.

"Our mission was a success," I answered.

I can only describe my elation as the most intense satisfaction I had ever experienced. Later that day, I boarded a plane to San Francisco to visit with my good friend and Riaz's sister before going on to Florida; I had a triangle-fare ticket, which allowed me forty-eight hours in one of the destinations. When we walked into the house from the airport, the phone was ringing, and the answering machine was flashing. Bano laughed as she listened. I had told her all about my experience. It was Riaz on the phone and answering machine. He spoke with fierce acrimony, claiming he and the other guys had to be hospitalized. His sister laughed, called him a loser, and hung up.

Years later, at a wedding on Long Island, Riaz asked me to forgive him, and told me it was the best payback anyone had ever given him—one he definitely deserved. I smiled and accepted his apology, but as I write this, I realize I will not forget how disheartened I felt.

I do not subscribe to my father's philosophy that "Payback is a bitch," and go looking to vindicate myself from being wronged by others. All acts of unkindness are judged by a force mightier than ours. I don't seek revenge or vengeance anymore and certainly don't recommend this recipe to anyone. Sometimes, I still feel bad about that night, though I do feel a smile forming on my lips as I picture myself racing through Lucky's market all those years ago. My prank seemed innocent then, but I shudder to think of the numerous repercussions I could suffer today.

Eating those brownies filled with Ex-Lax could have made those boys sick; they could have pursued me with an even nastier trick—just read the papers. So, I wouldn't do it again. But I'd be lying if I didn't say that I'm glad I did it; it changed my life, though not as much as it could have. I had reached a fork in the road, and instead of eating with the fork and nourishing myself, I chose a direction—only one.

Now, there should be some kind of Good Boy Brownie recipe, don't you think? After all, most boys are good, and they should be rewarded. Of course, Good Boy Brownies are suitable for girls, too. So here is a recipe from Betty Crocker and Nonnie, my husband's grandmother, for Good Boy Brownies:

≈

Good Boy Brownies

Ingredients:

2 squares unsweetened chocolate (2 ounces)—I prefer milk chocolate, but you can use either.

⅓ cup butter or shortening

1 cup sugar

2 eggs

1 cup flour

1 teaspoon baking powder

1 cup broken nuts (optional)

1 teaspoon salt

Preheat oven to 350 degrees. Mix together flour, baking powder, salt, and nuts (if you are using them). Melt together the chocolate and butter in either a double boiler or microwave. Beat in sugar and eggs, then slowly add dry ingredients. Spread into greased 8-inch or 9-inch pan..

*** TIP: Pam can be used in place of shortening, but you have to spray a little more than you normally would. Spray closer to the pan for thicker coverage.

Bake for 25-30 minutes, depending on how you like the texture of your brownies. You will get a gooier brownie by baking for less time.

*** TIP: I serve brownies warm with icing melting on the top or with a scoop of ice cream.

LAYER 7

Eggplant Parmesan and FU

"Human action can be modified to some extent, but human nature cannot be changed."

Abraham Lincoln

I love the kitchen; I played house when I was a child. Aunt Margie worked at Sears when I was ten or eleven. Annmarie, my cousin, and I went to work with her to play in the housewares department. It was so cool. They had three or four model kitchens fully equipped with utensils, pots, and pretend food. We'd play house for hours there.

Before that, I begged for a Suzy Homemaker oven. I made pizza using ketchup and an English muffin with Parmesan cheese, and cooked it under the 60-watt bulb that was the oven's heating element. Soon, I graduated into my mother's kitchen, concocting such experiments that only a loving parent would eat.

Food had always been intriguing to me. There is a power in knowing that a pleasing meal prepared lovingly will remain with a person long after it is digested. It is not uncommon to recall what you were eating at a special or even crucial incident. Our cellular memory has taste buds. I enjoy eating out, then going home and recreating it by memory and taste. It is never the same, but my own modifications make it mine.

Sometime in the late '70s the girls I hung out with were dating "surfers." They were a wild group of tanned beauties who liked to party and surf. They were into some strange stuff—they drank little bottles of ginseng through petite glass straws, smoked clove cigarettes, and listened to Bob Marley, who was a Rastafarian. They were serious about their sport, traveling to remote islands in the winter and surfing by the light of full moons in coveted spots they had their own names for, like the bowl, flies, and threes. There on the untamed beaches of Long Island's western Suffolk County, they ruled. They hung together, drove BMWs, trucks, Capris, and Woodys, and wore Patrick sneakers.

I was fascinated by their cult-like lifestyle. Their eating habits in particular captured my attention; they were mostly vegetarians. I had never cooked or eaten strictly vegetarian, but being a lover and mass consumer of vegetables myself, I embraced the challenge and, eventually, the lifestyle. The first person who made me feel omnipotent by virtue of my culinary knack in cooking Eggplant Parmesan was my friend Paul or "Fu" (pronounced foo), as he was called.

It was another engaging ritual the surfers practiced, all having nicknames like Shred, Dizz, and Moon Man. They referred to us girls as, "Chnicks" and admired our bodies with words like, nice "foil". For a while, I was dubbed "Snail Master"—hmmm.

Fu and I shared a unique unrequited palatability for one another. There was something about his silence that I understood. So when his cousin committed suicide, I devoted myself to the circumstance—an opportunity to create a meal that would serve as a vehicle for comfort and distraction to all of our confused and aching spirits. I felt compelled to aid in the healing process in the only way I knew how.

Perhaps I am just an old-fashioned girl; the way to a man's heart is through his stomach.

In retrospect, I believe I chose Eggplant Parmesan not only for Fu, but because it symbolized with its layers of ingredients the depth of our fear and sorrow—personal layers burdening our souls. I hoped as we ate through tiers of cheese, tomatoes, and eggplant, that everyone would experience a bit of healing.

Fu never said thank you, but he looked deeply into my eyes and nodded his gratitude. That small acknowledgment sealed our friendship and my acceptance into his environment, and it touched my heart, Fu was not an emotional guy, yet he laid his head on my shoulder for a moment, and I knew how deeply he was hurting. To this day, when I see an eggplant or create this dish, I think of him. I believe in coming full circle in life; therefore, I name this recipe for Fu. After all, his reception gave me confidence.

Awakening in the early '80s, I began my understanding of death in all its finality—all its mystery and my hope in its promise of life beyond our existence. It was the only way I could absorb why people died before their lives were lived, believing then that they could come back as new people or as angels if they had lived out all their lessons on Earth. I chose that time to embrace the possibility of life after death because our close-knit group lost too many members. How else could I find comfort in death when it arrived so early for some?

When Stevie ended his life in his sister, Kit's hammock in the back yard of their waterfront home, it was as though a great tsunami swept us away. He took his shotgun, of which he was proud and fond (he had admired many a goose through its sights), and then turned it on himself. I remember sitting next to him the night before he died; there were several of us at a long table outside The Post Stop restaurant. I didn't know him well, and, in actuality, he scared me.

He was close enough for me to look eyes while he spoke. He longed to tell me about the high intelligence of geese and his complete knowledge of their awareness, and his need to educate me seemed to overwhelm us both. Stevie seemed altered and distracted, distant and out of reach, and at the time; I imagine; frustrated, anxious perhaps not; perhaps he was being called by a power greater than himself. I have felt the claws of desperation at my back; he was out of my league and even though I was familiar with this sense of desperation, it made me uncomfortable.

In retrospect, I wonder if he was just looking for someone to talk to. He seemed so filled with erudition, so hungry to expel his wisdom—which was so obviously over my head—that he needed to anesthetize himself to avoid the enormity of his inability to put it to use.

He was drinking a mimosa laced with Grand Marnier, and I could smell the scent of grass. He wore wire-rimmed glasses like John Lennon; they were colored, too, I think. His head was covered in strawberry-blonde hair, dried with sand, salt, and sea air. I remember trying to gaze past his glassy-eyed stare to see what was inside this person I'd raced down Dune Road with, side-by-side, in our Capris.

Stevie was three or four years older and many moons away from my oddly impregnable world. His surfer's goatee scared me. It conjured up thoughts of evil, which I have no explanation for. But to this day, the style makes me uneasy. I think it reminds me of photos of the Devil that I saw when I was a child. I looked down at his large feet, covered with the same strawberry-blond hair as his head, and noticed how they were wrapped into each other as if they were a puzzle.

"Nothing is real," he said as he pulled a fat, Hawaiian bud rolled loosely in bamboo papers from behind his ear. "Don't be fooled by the shit they tell you; it isn't real."

I watched him light the "spleef," inhaling almost half of it.

"Geese are the most intelligent species—smarter than man," he said.

To this day, I have a deep respect for geese, and it offends me that my husband and my husband's friends would shoot such a graceful, intelligent bird. To his credit and defense, he admires their beauty and grace, too, and he is able to separate himself from that somehow when he is hunting—a sport he was introduced to by his grandfather and father. I believe when he is engaged in the act of hunting, it creates the bond of those he loved and has lost.

"Geese—really?" I asked, looking at Stevie closely.

I saw little chance of conversing with him; he was light-years beyond most of us with his aptitude and philosophy, which seemed weird to me then. I smiled, stood, and walked across the street. I was not completely surprised, yet still horrified to hear the next day that he was dead.

If memory serves, Kit, his little sister, found his body. I know there was some note or some form of farewell, though its content escapes me, and my cellular memory of the pain surrounding that day keeps me from making inquiries. It was just too devastating to them; they were a close family. Kit reminded me of a beautiful, hip Pippi Longstocking, a character from a children's book I adored as a kid. She surfed and was in the circle by proxy; she could boogie on that board like nobody's business. Her spunk, joy, and verve kept me in awe of her. That day, however, with her unkempt hair dull with mourning, she seemed smaller and more doll-like than ever.

She came by Judith Powers, the shop where I worked, accompanied by Fu, her cousin, who was also a redhead. He, in contrast to her littleness, was powerfully built with piercing blue eyes, red-rimmed from his sleeplessness and partying. It was morning; they strained with disbelief that someone they loved, trusted, and admired could shake their world so irreparably.

I held my arms out to them. Kit let me hug her for a minute, then shook me off and went in search of Freddie, her surviving brother, who had been missing in action. We girls feared Freddie would join his brother, though I know now he would not have. Freddie was full of life, spirit, and his own wisdom, which didn't seem to burden him as Stevie's seemed to burden him. His sense of humor and little-boyish qualities made him irresistible to everyone. I think that characteristic saved him.

My friend and housemate, Liz, was the liaison between the dregs (an affectionate term for surfers), the locals (me), and the city people (her), though she eventually became a local. Liz, like me, knew food and drink could hold our crushed spirits together. It was the only action we could take; everyone felt helpless, wordless.

We decided I would make Eggplant Parmesan. Most of the diners were vegetarians, so it would be a safe dish. I didn't have a car then, so I rode my bike to the market to buy groceries while Liz hit the liquor store. We rearranged our small living room with borrowed tables and chairs so it would be intimate.

Rituals are essential tools for comfort and healing; though I had never created a dinner party for mourning people, I understood in my heart the need to bring them together for a hot meal that would take some time to consume. I also felt the importance of seating us close together, so even if we couldn't find the words to say, we would be communicating through the warmth of our bodies. These ingredients became the bond during the time when life was splintered and foreign to us.

Long Island's summers can be unbearable; humid air could burden the most youthful spirit. That day, the weather was heavy and overcast, like us. I returned from my shopping, put on a Danskin leotard, wrapped my waist with the white dishwasher apron (I had an ample supply from many restaurants my father had owned), and began my task, grateful to have one.

≈

Eggplant Parmesan

(Feeds up to 20)

Ingredients:

5 large, shiny eggplants (from the farm stand on Montauk Highway)

1 dozen Italian tomatoes

1 clove garlic

1 red pepper

1 onion

1 bunch parsley

1 bunch celery

Breadcrumbs

3-4 Eggs

Extra virgin light olive oil

Parmesan cheese (Locatelli)

5 cans Progresso crushed tomatoes

Salt

Pepper

Red wine

3 secret ingredients

2 – 1lb. chunks of Italian mozzarella cheese 5-6 Lbs. tomatoes (please insert this last ingredient under the cheese and allow an additional line before preparations)

Before preparing the food, you will need several level surfaces. Employ flat plates, baking sheets, or broiling pans. (Use your imagination.) Cotton towels, paper towels, or brown paper bags with no writing on them will be needed for lining and absorbing liquid from sliced and peeled eggplant.

Peel eggplants and slice as thinly as possible. Place one layer of slices on flat surface; cover with a few layers of towels or paper, no more than 3 layers. Cover top layer with paper and another plate or pan and put full cans, rocks, or anything to add weight to the top plate. The key to eggplant is to drain the liquid from it before you fry it. I make mine so thin that you can eat them like chips.

Since this layering takes a great deal of time, I suggest excellent music, conversation, or a movie to keep it from becoming tedious. The draining time is about 3 hours.

In the meantime, begin the sauce. First, quarter the tomatoes, then open cans of crushed tomatoes. Crack 4-6 eggs in a large, deep bowl, and pour a generous amount of seasoned Progresso Italian breadcrumbs (or you can make your own breadcrumbs) into a large, deep plate, about two cups to start, and set aside.

Slice all mozzarella cheese and set aside. Before sautéing, pour about 2 tablespoons of olive oil in a large saucepan. Slice some garlic into quarters, and rub the bottom of the pan with each piece, leaving the smashed pieces in the pan. Next, pour a light layer of salt over the bottom of the pan and let it sizzle a minute. Remove the pan from the heat, and add chopped onions, celery, and some pepper to taste, and sauté them until the onion resembles cellophane. Add a shot of red wine or balsamic vinegar to the pan; let it sizzle again, and follow with remaining vegetable ingredients. (I believe I used mushrooms for this dinner. If you do, you would now add them, sliced or chopped.)

While these ingredients are becoming acquainted, introduce fresh tomatoes one at a time; stir, wait for the sizzle, and keep adding until the juices of each piece of tomato are joined with the rest of the mix. Cover and sizzle for a count of 300. Remove cover, stir, and slowly add the cans of crushed tomatoes (also one at a time to avoid splashing). Cover, stirring often, maintaining a high enough temperature without burning. (Smoke is a good indicator that it's too hot).

***TIP: As you stir the sauce, use a WOODEN SPOON ONLY. (Metal is sacrilege to the delicate acids of the tomato, but you could also use plastic.) If you feel anything sticking or see it on the spoon, the heat is too high.

***TIP: Spray or oil your wooden spoon to keep it coated, and add small amounts of oil while stirring. Once you've added all the ingredients for the sauce, bring to a light bubble, then cover and simmer for as long as possible. The longer the sauce simmers, the richer the flavor.

***TIP: Sometimes tomatoes can absorb flavor from the other spices, and it is necessary to add additional seasonings. Taste the sauce frequently while cooking.

While the sauce was simmering, I covered the tables using Liz's linens. Liz had linens and other comforts the rest of did not possess. Then, I cut some wildflowers and put them into several small vases along the tables, careful not to let the flowers obscure each guest's view. To make sure, I sat in every seat. Paying attention to these kinds of delicate details make me feel more connected to each guest. It is important they know I have put thought and energy into their arrival.

I remember that while I was cutting the flowers, I was thinking about Stevie. I couldn't imagine how he could have had the courage to put a gun to his own head. It is only now that I wonder if it was courage or confusion and fear that motivated such an act. I have experienced desperation and been immobile; I just never felt so incomplete that I thought I would be better off not feeling at all.

Perhaps it is, as some say, the ultimate form of bravery; I certainly cannot judge. Poor Stevie, perhaps he confused fear with courage. Or maybe in his heightened state of acute awareness, it became painful to feel, painful to fit.

Liz took off in her silver Mustang, making the rounds to each surfing spot in search of Freddie. She really liked Freddie, and her heart was broken with his loss. It is agonizing to see someone you love hurt with such vigor and to feel disabled, unable to make the pain subside. Not long after Stevie's death, Liz and Fred moved in together and eventually got married. I believe Fred needed Liz's patience, love, and tenacity to move him through his grief. She absorbed his torment with compassion and humor. Liz's selfless love healed Freddie's heart, enabling them to progress. I sense Liz created a new venue for Freddie to live for, and we are all grateful to her. I worried that the pain Liz took on would hurt her if she had no release.

She is a strong woman, though I have seen her vulnerable side. Most of us understood her desire to settle down with someone she could count on, and Freddie was her choice. They are a good match.

While Liz was out, I continued to design a therapeutic environment to honor our friend's passing. Tomato sauce permeated the cottage. Its aroma served as a powerful aphrodisiac to the cohesiveness we strove to harbor within our wounded souls. I finished setting the table, showered, and made my way back to the kitchen. I felt reinvented and decided to make a salad to enhance the meal.

I rode my bike to the market and purchased ingredients for a Caesar Salad. When I got home, I washed and cut the lettuce, put it in the big, wooden salad bowl from the pantry and covered it with damp towels before putting it back in the fridge. I learned this trick from a chef at one of my father's restaurants. It keeps the lettuce crisp for hours.

***TIP: don't wet the towels too much, or it will have the reverse effect and make the lettuce soggy—and never put the dressing on before serving.

By the time I finished the salad, it was time to cook the eggplant. Frying is a slow undertaking. In those days, I would sip a glass of wine or champagne. I remember frying and mourning at the same time; it felt right to feel this way while cooking in this manner.

≈

Cooking the Eggplant

Beat 1 cup of milk into bowl with eggs. (have the bowl large enough to submerge the eggplant slice). Pour 1-2 cups of breadcrumbs mixed with salt and pepper onto a plate. Lightly bread a large plate to hold eggplant slices ready to be fried. Preheat oven to 375.

Use a large, deep frying pan; I don't use a skillet because I prefer a shiny or slippery surface. I used three frying pans because we didn't have a large one in the rental. Pour a mixture of olive oil and vegetable oil (I use coconut or canola), into the pan until it is about a quarter of an inch deep. While prepping the eggplant, turn the burners on very low so the oil will be ready at the same time as the eggplant. Stack all the eggplant on one large plate.

The counter lineup is: eggplant, egg mixture, breadcrumbs, lightly breaded plate to place eggplant in while waiting on stove, frying pans, baking pan (or broiling pan) lined with paper. (Here, I use brown paper bags with no ink; however, thin kitchen towels or paper towels will work fine.)

I use the hottest pan that is closest to me first. Coat the eggplant with egg, then dip it into the breadcrumbs, being sure to bread both sides.

***TIP: Test the temperature of the oil by splashing a drop or two of water into the oil. If it sizzles a little, it's perfect; if you have to jump back, turn it down.

Place eggplant into frying pan. Count on four per pan at a time. By the time every pan is filled, the first batch is ready to turn. The fried eggplant should be golden brown—not too brown, though. Place the finished eggplant on the paper bag to absorb excess oil. It takes about 30 minutes to fry all the eggplant.

Frying the eggplant, my heart had this aching feeling, a kind or heartburn without the indigestion. It wasn't for Stevie's lost life, though, of course, I was dismayed to be so near the death of such a young person; it was the longing I knew the living would feel.

Being raised a Catholic child, I was taught that suicide kept your soul from having peace. It would wander from purgatory, a place somewhere between heaven and hell, to Earth—like limbo, one foot here, the other somewhere else. I was taught that, to God, it was a sin to take your own life. Death is God's job. I don't know if I believe in "sin or purgatory", but it seems a great loss to take your life when perhaps you could have been helped.

Then again, perhaps it was God not supplying the help. This discussion confuses my own mind and goes round and round with what I feel and what I think. I envisioned Stevie seeing his life below him so clearly that he could reach out and touch it. But when he tried, he would find the clear bubble confines of his destiny a barrier between him and his life. I pictured him without the hallucinations youth deludes, the shock and the reality of what he'd done sobering him for all eternity. I shivered with my thoughts, though my body was moist with perspiration.

I never spoke of this to anyone. First of all, it was not cool then to be thinking about God; second, I thought I was kind of under the influence myself. Now, however, it seems like a very authentic visualization, though I don't believe God would punish us. My own reality is based on my belief that hell is the punishment we inflict on ourselves, like Stevie not being able to take back that split second it took to take his life—that split second that would redefine so many other lives. I know from experience that when I act impulsively, whether from an emotional place or under the influence of a few glasses of wine, afterward, when I am lucid, I wonder if I had thought first, perhaps the outcome would have been different. Live and learn.

I believe in spontaneity; I enjoy being free enough to exercise that right when it won't harm anyone—some things need to be thought through. In my youth, I was impetuous often to my own determent. But that is what growing is about. It has taken me forty-five years to grow up, and sometimes I still feel like a twelve-year-old. I certainly do relate to them.

While the eggplant drains, take the largest baking pan you have or one that will accommodate your ingredients without bubbling over. Turn off your sauce and stir it a few times, then ladle it into the baking pan. Use a generous amount of sauce, though it is okay to use less as long as the pan is covered completely. Put the first layer of eggplant in the pan, followed by a layer of cheese, then another layer of sauce; continue this process until all the slices are covered. I like to add an additional layer of cheese, then sauce, to the top, though this is optional. Take toothpicks and lightly poke them around the top layer to keep the cheese from sticking to the foil. Then, cover the pan with aluminum foil for the first 25 minutes of baking.

While the eggplant was baking, I rummaged through the music to enhance the ambiance I'd hoped to create. I chose music that was safe; I did not want to be mellow enough to be depressing or too upbeat. I played some of my favorites, first to keep me relaxed, and then added other selections for our guests. I noticed Liz had placed her large, brass bowl in the center of the table. It had become a centerpiece at many gatherings and was intended to attract Freddie so Liz could seat herself next to him. I felt myself smile; my heart fluttered at the thought of her using this small gesture to lure her lover to her. Taking one last look around and feeling satisfied, I returned to the kitchen. For the last part of the meal, I prepared

≈

Garlic Bread

1 large, soft loaf of Italian bread (Any loaf bread will do.)

4 cloves garlic

¼ cup of olive oil (the lighter the better)

Salt

Freshly grated Parmesan cheese

1 stick butter

*** If using fresh garlic use a press or slice cloves very thin

*** TIP save uneaten garlic bread to grind in a blender for homemade breadcrumbs.

Split the bread down the middle, though not in half. (Separate it just enough to flatten it.) Drizzle olive oil on one side of bread; spread with knife or pastry brush. Butter the other side of the bread. Peel the garlic cloves and cut them in half, then put 2 halves into the press and squeeze over the bread, spreading evenly on both sides. (Use garlic according to taste.) Sprinkle salt lightly on one half, cheese on the other (optional). Close the bread, and wrap completely in foil. Allow 2 minutes while in foil, then open the foil, spread the 2 sides under the broiler, and allow the bread to broil for a short minute. While the bread is broiling, I throw a quick dressing on the salad and toss it. I usually make my own, but you are welcome to use anything you like.

I removed the eggplant from the oven while the bread was warming. I uncovered it and took out the toothpicks. Sometimes it needs to be placed back into the oven for a few more minutes to melt the top layers of cheese completely. I placed two or three trivets (towels or potholders work, too) on the table and placed the eggplant in front of my seat so I could serve. Liz busied herself putting the rest of the meal on the table, including drinks, while glancing at the door, waiting for Fred's big, red truck to squeeze its way through our narrow, hedged driveway.

I expected the guests to stagger their arrivals. My roommates came first. John brought Shred and Finky. Jackie showed up later with Kit; they clung together for comfort. Fu showed up with his friend from the shipyard, and, eventually, Freddie came.

The gathering, awkward in its origin, holy in its mission, began. Slowly, seductively, the scent tantalized the senses, cajoling the hunger pangs to stir within. Habit took control; mechanically, wine and beer were served while enhancers found their way around the table, and, eventually, peacefulness began. I realize one meal cannot heal the haunted heart, but food fills some of the emptiness grief takes away.

I felt a callused hand on my bare leg; I served the eggplant. I turned to look at Fu.

"Here's to Eggplant Parmesan and Fu," he said and smiled. "What else matters?" he added.

"You mean Lu," someone said.

"Fu and Lu," he said.

I ambled straight into those watery, red-rimmed blue eyes, and at that moment, I couldn't think of one other thing that mattered to me. I surveyed our guests, and the table I had so carefully set unraveled; the food had played itself out. How fragile we are, I thought. We sat there for that split second; peace, like the fragrance inhaled deeply into our lungs, shared in this room filled with people recollecting the responsibility of their sorrow At that moment before we stood, before we exhaled, before we digested, our hearts memorialized this meal, prepared with intentions to restore our health, the pieces of our broken youth.

I have never forgotten the taste of that evening. I recall what mourning looks like and feels like, and try not to fear it; though I still don't like goodbyes. Mostly though, I will never forget our punctured innocence, our deflated joy and a summer that abducted our youth, releasing us into adulthood without supervision.

LAYER 8

She She Lu's Scampi

"Do not neglect to show hospitality to strangers, for by doing that, some have entertained angels."

Hebrews 13:2

When I met my husband, Chris, I was preparing to leave California for the familiarity of my home on Long Island. Belonging to California as I hoped I would proved to be difficult; I was homesick for my ocean and the quaintness that was home.

I met Patti, my mother-in-law-to-be, before I met my husband. She introduced us without our consent. I wanted nothing to do with a man; my heart was in tatters from the last one. But she smuggled him in under my nose.

Patti's intuition was powerful; we clicked and began dating the following week. Our progression was rapid, though with some trepidation on my part. We met on September 18, Patti's birthday and my father's; we became engaged in January. Life's crazy-fast sometimes when you're trying to go slow!

I invested little time building close friendships; working as much as I could to pay off some debts and to support my dog, Rja, and myself. Rja was my best friend. I got her at the pound when Eric dumped me; he was the guy before Chris. Shortly after Rja and I became a couple, we were asked to leave the complex we lived in. I had a difficult time keeping her, paying exorbitant prices for weekly boarding; she and I slept in my Volkswagen some nights.

I found a foster home for her, but when I stopped in unexpectedly, I saw that she was being mistreated when she barked. One evening, I dressed her as a child with a scarf over her head and smuggled her into a cheesy motel in Santa Monica. For a while, we had settled with a friend, at Lise's home in the San Fernando Valley.

Lise is Eric's sister, and when she went to Japan, he liked to stop by and cry on my shoulder about his latest girlfriend—not the most fun I ever had. It was not so bad until her dog died, and although it was not my fault, I let Eric convince me Lise would blame me, not the bone she had gotten from the trash. So, I packed us up; we lived between the car and with friends when it was possible. Thankfully, when we became involved, Chris helped me pay the dog deposit on the apartment I had been saving for, and we had a home. In many ways, Chris was my knight in shining armor—and still is.

Chris had lots of friends, and Terry McQueen was the first one to take me under her wing, so to speak, and make me feel welcome. With her assistance I pulled off my first dinner party. Chris had never had a birthday party beyond his first! This was inconceivable to me. He loved my cooking and so I prepared and served Shrimp Scampi, Fettuccini Alfredo, and Caesar Salad to thirty people in our 900–square-foot cottage.

I had met some of his friends, but I was definitely still an outsider. Some of the girls were petty because I'd come in from the outside to steal a highly desirable bachelor. After the dinner, though, I was accepted by most of his real friends.

That petite beach house fed and bonded us to each other. Many fond memories originated there—our marriage and the birth of our first son. I loved living there and was disappointed when we were forced to move after the property had been sold. Our second child was born in Santa Monica. It was a wonderful experience, we brought him to our cozy, peach-colored home. We moved before his first birthday. Things turned out as they were supposed to; where we live is perfect for our boys, and, certainly, our home here has brought us more joy than any place could.

≈

Scampi

180 large, uncooked shrimp with shells

***TIP: Depending on the guests, I allow 6-8 shrimp per person.)

2 large sticks butter (salted)

1 cup light olive oil

5 cloves garlic (minced or finely chopped)

2 large, sweet onions

8 ounces white wine

2 bottles clam juice

Terry headed for the liquor store while I went to Santa Monica Seafood—the best fish market around. Patti's neighbor, Rosemary, works for SMS, so my shrimp were hand-picked and waiting for me. I also purchased fresh Italian bread and two bottles of clam broth. I chatted with the cashier about my large order and left with my booty. On the way to Boys Market in the Marina, I stopped and picked up a new top to wear at a boutique in Playa Del Rey. Then, I purchased ingredients for the salad and the Fettuccini Alfredo.

≈

Fettuccini Alfredo

Recipe for 6 (I multiplied this recipe by 5 to increase.)

6-8 tablespoons butter

3 tablespoons olive oil

1 cup unsweetened whipping cream

4-6 cups fettuccini noodles, cooked (Rinse in cold water or let stand in it if you won't be using them immediately.)

1 cup grated Parmesan cheese (Locatelli)

Salt and pepper to taste

1 pound thinly cut sliced Prosciutto

2 cans leisure peas (I like Green Giant in the silver can.)

Nutmeg (optional)

Caesar Salad

3 heads Romaine lettuce (allow 2 people per head)

1 egg yolk

Minced garlic

Parmesan cheese

Olive oil

Anchovies minced to death

1 teaspoon French mustard

1 cup croutons (homemade if possible)

I took all of my purchases and ingredients back to our Victorian Cottage on Fourth Street and unloaded in the red zone. I had so many packages and so little countertop that I had to use the washer and dryer for extra surfaces. I precooked the fettuccini noodles, Terry called.

"Hey, how's it going?" she said. "I got champagne, wine, beer, paper plates, utensils, cups, and napkins. I'll pick up the ice cream cake from Carvel on the way. Do you need anything else? Chris has no idea how lucky he is! See you later!"

Terry was generous with her friendship as well as her time and money. She was not full of herself the way I imagine celebrity kids could be. We were the same in that we missed our fathers. She was fortunate that her father had left her so wealthy with love and money. If you were to watch an old Steve McQueen movie, you could see where Terry looks a lot like her father.

After we discussed our outfits and I deveined the shrimp, I thought about the look on Chris's face. He was out of town, so he knew nothing about our plans. He traveled with his work, so we had weekends unless I went with him, which I did on occasion. I knew he would get a kick out of the party; he was such a kid at heart.

Prewash and cut the lettuce; put it into a bowl and cover it with wet paper towels and a few ice cubes to keep it crisp.

My mother called for directions and talked about the seriousness of the relationship as I minced a ton of garlic and chopped onions and parsley. My eyes were watering, and I sniffled so much that she

146

thought I was crying about Chris and me. As we talked, I set out several small bowls, pulled out my wok, which I would use for both recipes, and continued to prepare the remaining ingredients so all I would need to do later was cook.

Linda, Chris's sister, came with the flowers I ordered and the two large vases. She was excited and couldn't wait for the party. Linda is crazy for her little brother. It was close to four, so I needed to shorten the visit and take my shower.

As I showered, I thought about my father and all he was missing. I was engaged to be married to this man he would never meet. His daughter would walk down the aisle at his dream wedding without him. My tears, which flowed freely in the shower's stream, mingled on my cheeks. I still felt such a sense of disbelief, as though at any minute, he would call me on the phone.

I looked at my lovely, diamond engagement ring and was moved by one man's love, while saddened by the loss of another's. I found myself crying more often with the reality of his absence and the slim chance I would ever see him again. I took a deep breath and snapped myself out of it, put on mascara and lip gloss and blew my hair dry.

For Christmas, I bought myself black Guess jeans and wrapped them up for Chris with a card that said, "These are really a gift for you because you get to enjoy seeing me in them." (Oh, those 24s!) My red tank top matched the red and white apron my nani crocheted for me, and I was set to go. I never cook or serve without an apron; it's the costume for the ceremony.

Our living-sleeping area held the banquet table used in the trade shows. The fire crackled in the fireplace, warming the tiny room. I laid a lace tablecloth belonging to Chris's family over the rectangled surface, carefully arranging flowers at the head of the table, which reached into our bedroom. Terry would be here soon. She dropped off the liquor and supplies while I dressed, and went home to ready herself. Terry liked to be on time—sometimes early—so I was relieved she would be there when people came; I hadn't met everyone yet. I chose music stacking albums, allowing for mood change as the evening progressed; music is an extension of the meal.

Terry and Jerry, her fiancé greeted our guests and brought them into the kitchen to see me, the chef-in-progress. I greeted and received one-handed hugs and worked diligently with my thoughts in order and my wine glass at hand. Chris would be home any minute, so with all ingredients in place and ready to be transformed into our dinner, I waited to greet my man—a posse of butterflies in my stomach. Moments later, Chris arrived to SURPRISE! It went perfectly! I have a framed picture of the greeting.

Back in our kitchen, I rocked to Steely Dan while I prepared the Scampi.

In a large pan (a wok is excellent, but even a large frying pan will do), sauté the butter with the garlic, onions, and parsley, sprinkling about a ½ teaspoon of salt and pepper to seal the taste. Add the wine, more butter, and the shrimp; cover, and then lower the flame. (I borrowed another wok so the food would come out together, along with two large chafing dishes from Nonnie, Chris's grandmother.) In the second wok, melt butter on low-medium heat (lightly browning). For the Fettuccini, add about ¾ of the cup of cream, and raise the heat until it boils rapidly for about 3 minutes.

***TIP: You should see large, shiny bubbles.

Reduce heat; add Prosciutto, peas, and noodles, tossing vigorously with a wooden fork. Add the rest of the cream a little at a time—about 4 additions. If you choose to use nutmeg, which I don't, add it here. Pour it into the chafing dish, put Scampi in the other, and then toss the famous Puglisi Caesar at the table to the oohs and ahs of the crowd.

Preparing a Caesar in front of a crowd:

STAND TALL! You will need a large, wooden salad bowl (bigger is better), wooden utensils (spoon and fork), the salad ingredients mentioned earlier, several small chafing dishes, and a mortar (the end of a fat butter knife will work). First, pour oil, vinegar (a dash), and mustard (a teaspoon or to taste) over anchovies in bottom of bowl. Using the mortar, mush, crush, and create a paste with these ingredients. Add the egg yolk, beating constantly with a fork. Depending on how much lettuce you will add, use a cup of dressing to serve 10 people (Double it to accommodate larger recipes; you can save extra dressing). Add lettuce, tossing with great gestures, and be dramatic! Finally, top with the croutons. (Make you own croutons with leftover bread. Prepare it garlic-style or plain, then heat, and cut into small cubes. Croutons can be frozen, too.) Sprinkle a generous amount of Parmesan cheese along with fresh ground pepper, and serve. I squeeze the juice of one lemon over the salad just before I add the dressing for extra zest, but this is optional.

Don't forget the garlic bread!

Smear three loaves of Italian bread with blended butter, olive oil, minced garlic, and garlic salt (serves 30). Preheat broiler, and just after salad is served, have someone put loaves under the broiler for about 2 minutes or until lightly toasted. Slice, and serve in breadbasket.

I enjoy serving. I like the attention; it's like being on a stage. After the last drop of food (they ate every morsel!), I sat on Chris's lap and tasted my creations from his plate. I rarely eat my own cooking; I'm usually too full from tasting.

After I cleared away some of the scattered plates and chafing dishes, I opened the freezer to get the cake. To my horror, there was no cake. I had inadvertently stuck it in the fridge while retrieving something from the freezer. I held my breath and opened the fridge; my eyes fell on lumps of cake swimming in soupy ice cream. Oh, well, I thought, and I stuck candles in the remaining lumps and handed everyone a spoon and a straw. We sang *Happy Birthday* amid tears of laughter and pats on my future husband's back.

"You guys are perfect together. She's just the woman for you!" Grant, his best friend, said while hugging us so hard we feared the re-arrival of our meal.

When the last guest left, I surveyed the kitchen. There was nothing unused in any drawer, cupboard, or shelf. That was my indicator the party was a success. My sweet man pulled me to him, kissed me tenderly, and told me he had never been happier or felt more loved. "Back at ya," I said. Then I turned on the stereo to Boz Scaggs and rocked my way through the cleanup.

LAYER 9

Honeymoon Halibut

"Success in marriage is more than finding the right person;
it is a matter of being the right person."
Rabbi B.R. Brickner

We spent nineteen days touring the Hawaiian Islands; it was a honeymoon designed by the Goddess of Love. It was perfect. We passionately consumed mass quantities of raw oysters, chased with Bloody Marys and each other! Heaven! When we despairingly boarded the plane to come home, I felt a sense of fear that we would never be afforded the opportunity to come so close to ecstasy as during those nineteen days.

On the ride home, I vowed that we would always consume each other as though we were starving. I knew I was being naïve, but I was dedicated to creating the space for our love to continually unfold, which I have—well, we have—even when it was really, really hard. Perhaps that sounds corny, but I ask you, what great love story doesn't have a small element of corniness to it?

I asked a young girl I know who is sixteen what she thinks love is; she said she didn't know. She did want to know what I thought it was. I thought for a moment, feeling pressured to come up with a brilliant answer. Here is what I concluded: Love is a process, committed to finding light in the dark, and being willing to keep looking when your flashlight is out of batteries. It's about coming to a fork in the road and eating with the fork instead of crossing the road that may take you away from a place you can never come back to. It is seeing your husband asleep after twenty years and even though you were angry with him earlier, you still get that pang of love and desire in your stomach. It is knowing you do not want to live without that person, no matter how hard you have to fight to stay together. It is respecting the commitment even in a photo finish.

Somewhere in my life, I acquired the notion that romance was spurred by passionately planned, detailed meals, which is what I began creating in my head before our plane touched the ground, officially ending our honeymoon.

All feminism aside, I like taking care of people, and my husband is a VIP. I have always collected particulars about the people I infuse into my assemblage, recalling them when I wish to remind someone how important he or she to me. This is a habit I still maintain—and one that has blessed me with so many long-term relationships that I would be satisfied if I never added to my extended, yet intimate, group of loved ones. It is this habit that inspired me to create our first meal as a married/honeymooning couple: Honeymoon Halibut. Here is the recipe as well as the inspiration; I hope you will enjoy the process and the meal as we did.

≈

Honeymoon Halibut

2 fresh halibut steaks

4 beefsteak tomatoes

1 bunch cilantro

2 shallots, chopped

2 tablespoons capers

1 ripe avocado

2 cloves garlic, minced

1 tablespoon each salt and pepper

Dash of Tabasco to taste

Lemon juice to taste

Butter to taste

Sprinkle of garlic salt

Cucumber Salad (accompaniment)

4 cucumbers

2 tablespoons rice- and red-wine vinegar

2 tablespoons olive oil (mild)

1 thinly sliced Maui onion (Any sweet onion will be good.)

2-3 tablespoons sesame seeds

2 cups white rice

Soy sauce to taste

I prefer buying fresh halibut if possible; it is not always feasible, so choose a place that has exceptional frozen fish, like Trader Joes.

I learned about halibut while I was camping on the tip of Baja with a group of surfers I'd befriended. The boy I was dating spent every moment amid the surf, like his comrades. I wandered the beach. A few days in a row, I would see a person in the surf. I decided to get closer; seeing it was a young Mexican boy, I made my presence known. The guys were so far out in the surf that I wanted to be sure I didn't dally with any strangers who could harm me. Intrigued by his backward movements in the shoreline surf, then quick reflexes in spearing a fish, I moved closer to him so he would know I was interested in what he was doing. I spoke little Spanish, but he managed to comprehend my curiosity. With animated movements, he tried to explain his actions.

Eventually, he took me by the hand and led me into the water. He instructed me to imitate his movements, which were shuffling his feet slowly while stepping backward in the shallow water. After a few moments, he pointed excitedly to a fish that was uncovered by my feet, and he quickly speared it.

He held it up and said, "Alibut, sí?" His pronunciation was quite different, but we understood one another perfectly. He could not have been older than ten. His face was angular, deeply browned by the sun, and he had large, black saucers for eyes. He smiled a perfect row of white teeth and nodded happily.

He showed me a net bag, mended in many places. He gestured for me to look more closely, and I leaned down and saw it was filled with many fish. To the left of it, he had a straw basket with lobsters in it.

"Do you sell to your people, denaro?" I said rubbing my fingers together in the money gesture. I stumbled on my Spanish. I was thrilled at his booty. He smiled, "Si." His face was filled with pride, and I thought how differently the children I am acquainted with are, spending money on games and entertainment. Different worlds; not better or worse, just different.

"Nombre?" I asked, forgetting the proper way to ask his name.

" Miguel. Y tu?"

" Luann," I smiled.

He nodded, "Muy bonito."

I don't know if he meant me or my name, but I was touched and happy to make his acquaintance.

I said "Si," though I had never seen a live halibut before. It was wide, very flat, and dark gray. It could have been any kind of fish for all I knew. He seemed so sincere, and I trusted him.

He led me down the beach to our campsite and began preparing a fire, gathering bits of wood and dry seaweed. Then, he motioned to me for with his hands for some ignition; he wanted to light the fire. I found a lighter and handed it to him. He let the fire burn hot for about five minutes and then put a wad of wet seaweed on top, causing it to sputter and smoke. He placed the fish on the seaweed for a few minutes, turning it once. With a knife, he removed the fish and dropped it on a rock.

He pulled me close enough to the fish so I could watch his precise movements as he peeled its melted skin back, baring its flesh. He then sliced it down the middle, exposing its skeleton, which he removed in one swift movement.

"Eat, si?" he said, gesturing for me to taste the fish. I had never eaten fish without lemon, or heavily seasoning it to kill the taste. But I didn't want to insult his cleverness, so I took a bite, using my fingers as he did. It was marvelous.

In the next few days, he taught me how to spear a lobster and cook it in a seaweed pool; he carried down an old, tin can one day and filled it with seaweed and seawater. He put the lobster on top with an onion and covered it again with more seaweed and a piece of wood he found on the beach. It cooked in no time and was the best lobster I have ever eaten. After that, I ate halibut often, though until my Honeymoon Halibut, it never tasted as delicious!

I was young and eager to please my husband; I don't remember one boy friend who made me feel so special and loved; my husband was the first, and I wanted to show him how much I loved him.

From the moment we began dating, he courted me. In the past, I was always chasing the wrong guys—bad boys who would love me and leave me, taking slivers of my heart and confidence with them. He was different, and this scared me initially. I fought his attentions for a while. I am only human, though, and in receiving flowers—orchids, lilies and roses—I couldn't help but softening. Plus, he played with my dog, Rja, and walked her.

He paid for her to go to the emergency room after her spaying site became infected; he just called the hospital and gave them his charge card over the phone—no questions asked. He was in Arizona at the time, traveling for work, and it was after 11 when I called and woke him crying frantically.

He was and is always generous and so quick to smile that endearing smile; I still melt. He laughs so hard while he's telling a joke that I fall apart, and he cries at sad movies, though he's as manly a man as they come. I know how lucky I am; I never forget to be thankful. He is the sexiest man I have ever seen; even Brad Pitt, whose smile charms me, can't hold a candle to his. He has great legs, a great ass, and a soul that has been kissed by angels.

Don't get me wrong—he's stubborn, sometimes unyielding, and opinionated, and sometimes he's a butt head. But he loves me when I am one, and he's the most loyal husband and father I have ever known. If I sound naïve here, I don't care; we as a society can afford to be naïve about some things, especially love in all its imperfections.

Honeymooning was still in my energy field. I waited for him to leave, then drove to the fish market. I chose the two steaks, which were medium width. After that, I went into Marina del Rey to Boy's Market because they carried better produce and more specialty items. While I purchased the other ingredients, I admired my sparkling, new jewelry—proof that I was, indeed, a married lady and on the journey of a new life with my husband.

In retrospect, I can feel my smile, contagious to everyone I encountered. I remember captivating strangers with my enthusiasm as a newlywed, knowing everyone must feel my joy. Driving home with my ingredients gently swaying in their bags, singing to Al Green's, Let's Stay Together, I concocted variations of my recipe. I visualize food much the same way as I write in my head, editing ingredients and words, replacing and imagining how they will look and taste long before I put them into action.

At home, I carried my parcels into the house, ready to go. I felt like a director spreading my ingredients out, putting them in their order of appearance, so to speak, my refrigerator acting as the "green room." I inspected my halibut in its paper wrapping, smelling the steaks and touching them for any slimy or filmy feeling. Seeing I had chosen well, I washed and patted them dry. I rubbed them with garlic and laid them in a Pyrex dish. (I do not like to put fish in metal in the fridge because I worry that the metallic taste will be absorbed into the fish.) Squeeze a whole lemon on fish, cover it with cellophane, and put it in fridge for later.

***TIP: To squeeze a lemon without spraying your eye, cut in half and wrap in cheesecloth, gauze, or a paper towel, wrapping it tightly around the half as though preparing to wring it out. Squeeze it, turning it around and around until it is emptied of juice.

I washed and cut the tomatoes, preparing to dice them small for a salsa sauce I would put on top of the fish once I grilled it.

I remembered my friend Alain, who treated his foods like they were children, delicately handling and placing each item he would use for his recipes. He taught me to rub a few drops of Crisco onto the grill so it would burn off and the fish would not stick.

I have been so blessed to learn from a myriad of chefs and great cooks through the years of my life spent in restaurants. I am always watching, listening, and respecting the creative gifts and theatrical presentations of foods; mostly, it's the tips I pay attention to. If I see someone do a clever step, I memorize it; the same goes with me if I see that I could do something more effectively.

Cut the tomatoes, finely scraping the juices and seeds into a medium-sized mixing bowl.

*** TIP Tomatoes and onions require sharp blades; you can take them to any market that has a meat department, and if the butcher is not busy, he can sharpen them for you. I own Henkels knives, but recently, I was given a Ginsu knife at a demonstration, and it is the sharpest (and stays sharp) knife I have ever used! Who knew?

Chop the cilantro, garlic, and shallots, and add them to the tomatoes with the capers, salt, pepper, and Tabasco sauce.

I don't use a food processor to make salsa because it makes the tomatoes seem foamy, and I believe the speed of the blades makes them ferment (My husband calls these superstions "Lu-isms.") This mixture joins the halibut in the "green room" (fridge). I peel the cucumbers. Though I know the skins are edible when scrubbed clean, it ruins the texture of this salad, in my opinion. Slice the onions thinly, adding them to the cucumbers, vinegars, olive oil, and sesame seeds, and refrigerate.

Since I grew up on Uncle Ben's white rice, I still use it for "perfect rice every time," but use what you prefer. If you stink at cooking white rice, or are pressed for time, buy a quart from a Chinese or Japanese restaurant. Prepare the rice minutes before serving, so it is light and fluffy.

I add soy sauce and garlic-caper sauce into the water after it boils. This is made by mincing 2 cloves of garlic to every tablespoon of capers with liquid—mince or chop. Refrigerate in a container with a tight lid, and it lasts quite awhile. When rice is finished, add the butter, and let it sit with the lid on while you put the other foods on the plates.

While the foods were marinating, I showered, put on a short, sexy dress, set the table with candles, crystal, silver, and china, (wedding gifts) and a single rose from our garden, and waited to welcome my husband home for the first time. This was my first time using these wonderful gifts; I was so excited.

I called my husband, who said he was leaving, which, depending on traffic, gave me about forty-five minutes.

This first evening in our tiny, Victorian beach house as husband and wife was deserving of the utmost attention to detail right down to music and the scent I chose to wear, which was Fracas. Moments before my husband walked in the door, I turned the ringer on the phone off, put the rice water on to boil and stood in the doorway poised and ready to receive my man.

We enjoyed a cocktail while I checked the fire on the grill and prepared to cook the halibut. I put on my apron (I love aprons; I think they're sexy), sliced the avocado (not too thin), and put it back into the fridge.

Make the rice while you put the fish on the grill. Do not put it in the center unless you are prepared to stand there with a timer; otherwise, the outside burns and the inside is raw, unless you like it that way. I figure 6-10 minutes on each side, depending on the thickness of the fish.

***TIP: If you push the fish with your finger, it should react like a marshmallow when squeezed, breathing back to its original shape.

Move the fish from the grill to the plate, spoon on salsa, and top with avocado slices. The cucumber salad blends nicely with the fish's flavors, so I serve it on the same plate, though you are welcome to put it into a separate dish. I also like to serve the rice on the same dish, though not under the fish because it gets mushy; again do your own thing here.

I poured my husband's beer into a chilled glass from the freezer; do this by rinsing a glass inside and out, and place it in a secure spot in the freezer for at least a half hour. I poured myself a glass of Sauvignon Blanc. We toasted to the promise of "us" and we ate our first meal as a married couple in our home. These are precious moments; savor them while you eat them up!

LAYER 10

Something's Fishy, but not the Cioppino

"The way to a man's heart is through his stomach"—that and hours of kissing in my '69 Volkswagen outside the Brentwood Inn, I think. Cioppino is my husband's favorite dish. He ordered it in San Francisco the night he proposed. I tasted it, modified it, and made them both mine.

During the summer of 1987, Liz and Fred came from Westhampton Beach with their eighteen-month-old son, Kevin. They were the epitome of the American family. Beautiful Liz, tall, blonde, and blue-eyed; Fred, handsome, tall, blue-eyed, strawberry-blonde; and their baby made a gorgeous combo. They drove up in a Volvo, looking like an advertisement for Perfect Life, and, for a while, it was.

I met Liz when she transferred to our high school from Manhattan. She was the envy of many local girls, dating the hunky Aram Terchun, my good friend Rosemary's brother. She was everything we "country girls" were not. With her father's convertible Bentley parked in the lot and living in one of the most beautiful homes on the beach, she had an edge. Aside from her beauty, she was cultured and elegant in a wholesome way. What was not to envy? We were in P.E. together, and I began a conversation with her; the rest, as they say, is history.

It is customary to cook for the hostess; Liz and I enjoyed each other's creations. I made Cioppino. Cioppino is a soupy fish stew—a meal for people who enjoy eating with their fingers and slurping its delicate broth.

≈

Cioppino

2 large Dungeness crabs

***TIP: Have the fish store crack and clean them.

1 pound cherrystone or littleneck clams (soaked and cleaned)

1 pound large shrimp (If serving hearty eaters or 6, use 2 pounds.)

1 pound baby scallops

1 pound black mussels (small)

1 stick butter

1 cup olive oil

1 large, sweet (Maui) onion

3-4 whole garlic cloves, sliced paper-thin

1 bunch Italian parsley

2 chopped celery stalks

3 large cans whole tomatoes (Progresso) or 8 very ripe Italian plum tomatoes

16 oz. vegetable, beef, or chicken broth (I use Knorr's dried soup, but canned is fine.)

Fresh basil to taste (I use 3-4 leaves), cooked with oil and garlic

3 pinches fresh oregano

1 can tomato sauce (canned or homemade)

Wine is optional; I use 2 cups of white wine

Liz and I chatted in the fish market. She was concerned that Kevin hadn't been trying to walk since they left home. He was irritable and would only crawl.

"At home, he cruises like a wild man. I have to watch him every second," Liz said, her voice cracking a little.

At the market, Kevin was miserable. He tugged at one side of his head. We thought it was an earache from the plane. Frustrated,

Liz tried to comfort her baby. Poor Kevin cried all the way home. Freddie tried to reassure Liz.

"It's just the plane," he said. "His balance is off."

Freddie took Kevin to the park, hoping to distract him. We opened a bottle of wine, and I started dinner. Liz told me she thought something was terribly wrong. We drank the wine.

≈

Cioppino

In a large saucepan on high heat, melt the butter and olive oil; add sliced garlic, stirring constantly until lightly browned. Lower heat; add onions, celery, and parsley. I like to raise and lower the heat a few times so the onions also get lightly browned around the edges.

Add wine; cover, and let simmer for 5 minutes. Add tomatoes, broth, basil, oregano, and a teaspoon of salt. If you can, use kitchen scissors to cut the tomatoes in the pan. If not, scrape the juices into the pan from the cutting board. Cover and simmer on medium for 40 minutes. Devein the shrimp, and leave tails on. I bought this cool tool for deveining shrimp. You can use a knife, too. Insert the tool or knife at the bottom of the shrimp (the fat part); slide or slice along the spine, and pull out the vein.

***TIP: I cook shellfish in their shells to keep them from drying out. Cook them slowly to ensure tenderness.

Wash mussels, and remove beards with a sharp knife by holding the mussel in one hand and scraping the bearded side, lightly pulling beard out. Rinse scallops, and put them aside with the crab.

My son Sean's christening was Sunday; Liz could hardly wait to get it overwith so she could get her baby home. I understood completely. It is difficult enough to travel with your kids, stay in someone else's house, and be away from the normal schedule children that age need. But when your baby is sick and away from his or her own bed, it is sheer torture for everyone.

Put in crab for ten minutes; then add the shrimp, mussels, and cherrystones.

Kevin's misery became unbearable. We called our pediatrician, who suggested a decongestant to see if it would relieve the pressure in his ears. Poor Kev wouldn't even crawl by the end of the night; he just wanted to be held.

Add the scallops last, and turn the heat down to allow it to simmer for 5 minutes. I set the table with large, wooden bowls, nutcrackers, clam forks, and dishtowels for everyone to use as a napkin. My great-nani called these rags "Mopins." (The *i* has an *e* sound.) No napkin did her dinners service. I put a large shell bowl in the middle of the table with the hot, sourdough bread to soak up the soup. You can offer a spoon, but most of us preferred the bread-soaking method.

I served the Cioppino in a large soup tureen of Nonnie's; everything tastes good in Nonnie's bowl. We drank and ate a lot, but our moods were raw. As women, our intuition told us something was really wrong with Kevin.

That night, I got a fever of 104. My head hurt so bad that Chris called the doctor at three in the morning. We were all a little relieved, thinking maybe that was what was wrong with Kevin.

Sean's christening was beautiful. We had it at the Lake Shrine in Pacific Palisades. It reminded me of the Island of Avalon minus the mists. The Reverend Brother Ramonoda performed the service, dressed in his orange vestment; the ceremony was lovely and, thankfully, short. I got mixed reviews about my choice of location, but my husband and I were undecided about our religion at the time; this was nondenominational.

Liz and Fred left shortly after the reception, heading to Lake Tahoe. Liz took Kevin to the pediatrician, who told her his seemingly reversed walking process was normal, but not to Liz. Once they got home, she took him from doctor to doctor. Some of them actually told her she was overreacting.

Thankfully, Liz blew them off. A neurologist performed a CT scan on Kevin and found a tumor incased in a cyst in his head. It was a rare tumor; I don't believe many other child to date had suffered from one. We were devastated for days. Liz and I cried and talked on the phone. It was one of the worst times I can remember, and I held my baby every chance I got.

We prayed and pleaded with God to spare Kevin. There was a speck of light at the end of the tunnel because the tumor was encased in the cyst—it was localized. That poor baby had a surgery every few months for years. They almost lost him several times. If Liz had not trusted her mother's instinct and been persistent, who knows?

Today, Kevin is sixteen. He is a miracle.

Throughout this journey, Liz and Fred have become advocates and board members of the Brain Tumor Research Foundation. Liz speaks to families, counsels, and consoles.

That experience of making Cioppino alerted Liz that something fishy was going on with her baby. That dinner alerted us for the duration of our parenting, which, happily, continues on. Never second-guess when something seems wrong; trust your instinct, trust your intuition-it was given to you for a reason. Don't second-guess yourself because someone has a license or passed a test that you never took. You know when you know.

God bless you, all my friends, and thanks, God, for Kevin.

LAYER 11

Fond-a-u-Fondue

"The union of the family lies in love;
and love is the only reconciliation of authority and liberty."
Robert Hugh Benson

Divorce is so common that pretty soon, we'll be able to go to the market, get a coffee, do our banking, and file for divorce on the disposable vows aisle. It's a bad message. Marriage is work, no question. Divorce leaves a wake forever. To a child, it's second to death—maybe worse. True, death is final, but divorce is an ongoing string of little deaths. A new room in a new place compared to the security of the old room down the hall from Mommy and Daddy— no contest; no comparison.

If you get a divorce, put your children first. The missing ingredient in their emotional stability recipe is reconciliation—in any form. When you said, "I do," your promise extended to them.

I used to be more liberal in my thinking. I figured that I deserved to be happy, so, whatever I wanted, I should be able to do or have. It was and is an immature and selfish attitude. Sometimes I forget. I try not to. I do deserve happiness; we all do. It took a long time to learn this: I am happier when my kids are happy, and I have a lot of control over that happiness. It really is that simple. My kids count on my husband and me to keep the forever promise, which means we stay together even when it is so difficult that we can hardly stand it. Somehow that promise helps us find our way.

I dislike when my choices are taken from me; so do kids. It's about sacrifice, too—the kind that makes them sure of their values to you and to themselves.

I am not naïve; I understand there are circumstances in which a divorce is necessary. I do ask you to explore every avenue before doing this life-changing action. It brings up so many issues for kids, often not surfacing until much later. It demeans their ability to trust, and make good decisions, and it even hampers their ability to aspire to commit.

If you can't reconcile, manufacture a new vow: "We promise to keep you safe, loved, and cared for, together and apart." Create a place of extended love; blend in civility, even kindness, and bake at lower temperature so the cake can still rise and be iced without sinking from a violent move or loud noise.

Demand yourself to put their needs first, even when it feels like you are feeling compromised—even if your spouse is an ass. Your presentation will make all the difference to your child's healing and future ability to become a secure healthy adult, alone and in a relationship. Constantly check your behavior, and your motivation; a good attitude is contagious. Never give your power away; stay focused on your children's welfare; even when the butt head you married tries to trick you into old, negative behavioral patterns. "Smile though your heart is breaking," as the song goes. You can do this; after all, you are strong and the parent of amazing children—the future of our world.

Never, never take your vocation lightly.

Be kind to a stranger—piece of cake; be kind to your ex—hell, that's effort. We get crazy when we feel victimized or don't get our way. Divorce demoralizes rational adults; hurt and ego become weapons. Who likes having a promise broken? No one I know.

I still don't get why we don't educate our kids in school about real life; I don't mean sex and condoms. They could use an emotional first-aid class, a textbook, and a how-to guide: *Tips for Life and Recipes for Coping.*

What to do with the crazymakers we have as parents and relatives? If I had been given better ingredients to whip up my life, I would have avoided a lot of chaos. I get a little crazy when I remember what my brother and I dealt with when our parents split. I see it in the eyes of my kids' friends, in their fragmented existences, and I get sad.

I don't mean to judge or preach; perhaps it's experiences from past lives nudging me on. I just like kids, and I want them to be happy so they won't kill themselves or other people. This recipe is dedicated to some kids I love who are living with divorce, and to those I haven't met yet who suffer the fate of crazy parents.

When my friend Suz began to swim the treacherous seas of divorce, her kids' hearts became precious gems we fought to preserve. Her girls dealt in their own way. Somehow, we women "fix and move on"; our stuff comes out later.

Guys have to deal more with their issues; sometimes it's reversed. Sometimes issues don't get dealt with, and kids grow up into confused adults. There's no real rule, only survival. I knew more truthfully what it felt like for the girls because I am one. My pain from my parents' divorce re-emerged for me when I saw the desperation in their eyes and the darting of my own kids' eyes for a reassuring glance from me that this would not happen to them— seeing kids around them divorce like it was some new trend.

When our father left us, I was twelve; my brother was thirteen. Our parents had had a nasty physical fight. My father threw my mother at the fireplace—the only thing I ever saw my father build himself. It was a brittle, rainy February.

It occurs to me that my father left us twice in February: once for another woman and her children, and the last time, forever. The first time, he left in a silent rage only to return and ask to be let back in. My mother asked us what we wanted her to do. Letting him go was a hard choice to make; we loved him, but we hated him. At that time, it was about survival—our mother's and ours. So, with guilt and weighted hearts, we let him go.

His stuff was on the porch in sad heaps of melting memories. Looking back, I hardly recall my father living with us. I remember him sleeping there occasionally and using the bathroom. I recall certain television shows shown now on "Nickelodeon," and I envision him on our sofa on a Sunday or Thursday evening in the winter.

That last night, he stood looking at us through our bay window on the porch of our house. We sat on the hearth of the fireplace watching sadly as his stare penetrated our souls, his breath fogging the glass. He placed his hand on the window, tapping the glass with his ring as he often did to have us open the door when he came home late or early in the morning from work.

I wanted to jump into those strong, hard arms to make him stay, to erase the hurt. I knew with the wisdom of a grieving child that we were no longer a family. Never again would he enter our door with his key. The locks would be changed. There would be no man to run to if the "boogie man" came.

Though it was dark and rainy, his beautiful, blue eyes clouded over with tears; he turned, looked back once as if to say, "Please let me in," and then he walked away, arms loaded with his life—the things that at one time connected us to him.

His headlights faded from our view. He drove away from our lives, never to return in the same capacity. We were lost to him and him to us. When we were spent, no tears left to shed, my mother said, "What should we do?" She looked young and fragile with tearstains on her skin and blouse, her eyes swollen, her lip fighting not to quiver. It was one of the few times I remember my mother showing her vulnerability.

We couldn't eat, so we played Monopoly while my father unpacked his bags in another woman's house, and while he bounced her children on his knee, we haggled over Boardwalk and Park Place and slowly picked up the pieces of our shattered dreams.

Since his departures, I have never had a favorable dream about him; in contrast, he is always rather distant and put off by my presence. Although I cry to him to take me back as though I were a jilted lover, he turns his back on me. It feels odd and unnerving, and I cry out in my sleep.

Suz's kids were depleted, their situation contrasted by specific circumstances to my own childhood experience. Technology has changed; instead of him finding a woman in a bar as my father did so often, he found his new woman in a chat room. Similarly, another woman took their father from them.

He announced the split to his then- twelve-year-old daughter on their mother's birthday— a cruel and demonic revelation revealed by a heartless cad wearing their father's clothes.

I have no respect for anyone who behaves recklessly with emotions and lives. He hurt his kids, and that hurt me. If I were an Indian, I would have painted myself with war paint and done a dance to have his manhood fall from his body. Alas, I could only be there for them, as were my husband and children; we prayed for them all, including the cad, and listened to endless renditions of his abominable behaviors, one more shocking than the next.

True to the cad's form, John's dad forgot to call him on his birthday, and we decided to have a little surprise celebration to ease his disappointment; I am very big on celebrating the life we have.

I served Fondue, one of our favorite dishes when we were kids. It was one of the really special events my mom planned for us and our friends for special occasions. As I look back on this metaphor, serving food involving something raw and heating it to make it warm, I think all of life's ingredients are served through the recipes we choose for our survival. The very act of cooking is in itself a primitive way to involve people as the ingredient that binds two streams together. It is a confluence of putting out and taking in—a perfect yin and yang.

I suppose that's how this combination of stories and recipes came to be. For me, food feeds the soul, the mind, and body, therefore justifying and satisfying my hunger in perfect symmetry.

≈

Fond-a-u Fondue

2-4 cups peanut oil, depending on fondue pot size

***TIP: Peanut oil burns slow and clean.

1-2 pounds filet mignon (You can use a tender sirloin.)

1-2 pounds large, raw shrimp, deveined with tails removed

1-2 pounds chicken breast

*** This amount of food fed eight of us with some left over.

Teriyaki Dip

1 bottle honey-glazed teriyaki sauce

2 tablespoons sour cream

2-3 tablespoons catsup

1 teaspoon brown sugar

Orange-Lemon Marmalade Dip

1 jar each orange and lemon marmalade

1 teaspoon horseradish

1 cup frozen pink lemonade

Thousand Island Dressing with Garlic

1 cup mayonnaise (Helmans or Best Foods)

1 cup catsup

2 tablespoons sweet relish

1 tablespoon garlic in oil

Garlic Lemon Butter

1 cup lemon juice (Fresh-squeezed is best you can control the tartness.)

½ stick of butter

1 chopped onion

2 cloves fresh minced garlic (You can also use garlic in oil.)

I went to the market alone during the off-hours, thinking how John would always remember his father forgetting his birthday. I remembered that ache so well that I filled up with tears. I could see his eyes register disappointment, an emotion I was familiar with. That particular pain lessens through time yet easily surfaces anew with whatever jogs the memory of that incident.

I asked the butcher for six filet mignons (other cuts work, but this is my favorite) and four chicken breasts. I dabbed at my tears. The kindly butcher, feeling my pain, chose the freshest and largest shrimp for my recipe; he actually added a few extra. I chose my other ingredients, purchased balloons, and then went to order an ice cream cake from Baskin-Robbins. You really can't go wrong with a cake from B&R. I knew Suz couldn't have afforded this cake right now but that she would be comfortable with my good fortune at being able to do it for her. I thought about single mothers, my own and Suz. The burdens of motherhood are ominous. Mothers wear hard hats with heels, and I don't mean that to be a sexy visual, though I see the potential. We are contractors, supporting the beams that hold

181

the structure together after the foundation has been demolished. We are: the Red Cross, party planners, boo-boo kissers, mood detectors, beasts of burden, deflector shields, cheerleaders, rule enforcers, researchers, flowers, rocks, and so much more.

I reviewed my list, feeling somewhat soothed. I believed God had plans for the ice cream cake, which I chose not knowing the kind Johnny liked. I don't care what you believe in—God, the universe, little, green people—just believe in something higher, something sacred, or you may drown in your humanness. You may think you are driving alone, but you are only riding shotgun. It is a comfort to me knowing the two of us are in the cab of this monster truck capable of maneuvering through alleys as well as brick walls.

Pulling out of the lot, a pretty blonde woman holding her blonde daughter passed. I witnessed a sacred moment between them, faces snuggled together with their laughter like a song in my ears. I reflected on the love Suz has for her kids; it makes up for a lot they miss not having their dad. Her commitment is awesome; still, there is a void. We are meant to have mates; hers has not arrived yet, but just as she is searching him out, he, too, is searching for her.

I met Suz in 1992. Our kids were in kindergarten in the Canyon School. I had seen her around; I felt I knew her. Like a spy, I watched her with her son, Christopher, who is blind and autistic, and has an amazingly grounded soul. They were walking across the campus about ten feet in front of me. She had whispered something in his ear and he threw his head back and laughed so hard that she laughed, and so did I. I watched her guide him with her cane of love, touching him deeply with pure delight. Though they were in their own space, I could not bring myself to leave. I was drawn into it, and it changed me. They were fused to each other, joined at the heart, traveling to a holy destination—an exclusive journey of parent and child. I watched her cajole him while guiding his step, protecting him with her smiling laughter. It was a sight to behold, and I feel blessed to have witnessed such clandestine intimacy.

I knew from my limited experience of handicapped children that this woman carried a heavy load on her strong yet fragile frame. Her parcel was not a burden, though; that was obvious to the observer in me. I noticed her posture, feminine, firm, and pliable, and at that moment, I sensed a great sadness in her. I fought the urge to offer her my own tenderness; it seemed to me she was starved of it. I realized I was crying, silent and unnoticed.

So moved was I by this person that I made a pact with myself; I would find a way to know her. I would bear witness to that uncluttered love she fed her son on that day, and I would experience that light shining from the ends of her fine hair. I am passionate about my kids, and my husband and I hug them and love them every moment we can, but that relationship—well, it was virginal. I had no idea we would spend the next eleven years entwined in each other's recipes for living. I'm glad I listened to my intuition and trusted my instincts—a gift we women are taught to ignore by a society dominated by men. I love men, but I wish more women and men would trust that instinct bestowed to us in our mothers' wombs. It led me here, and it's a good place to be.

I got home and prepared the fondue pot, filling it with oil, and set out several dishes and small bowls, fondue forks, and skewers. I always use cloth napkins, or, even better, give everyone a kitchen towel because it can be a little messy with raw food and oil. I set the table, remembering an incident when John was about four, and I was driving home from the park with all of our kids in my old Volvo.

In my rearview mirror, I could see him looking at me. I observed his serious face but said nothing. When we got home, I unlocked the back door and opened it so he could get out and I could get my son out of the car seat. He stopped halfway out of the car and looked up at me.

"What is it John?" I asked, highly curious.

"I like your earrings," he said. "The pearl and the diamond next to each other like that—well, it's elegant."

"Elegant," I repeated to no one. I felt my ear, unable to remember what I was wearing. I had pearls on and a diamond in the second hole. I looked in the side mirror. He was right; it was elegant. After that, I felt good about myself all day.

Later that evening, Suz arrived with John. We hollered, "Surprise!" but Suz's kids are as honest as they come, and he confessed he could see the balloons through the window. John was wearing that delicious smile that feels reserved for me, and we could not all help but fall prey to his charm.

Our dinner was a blast. The conversation ranged from heartfelt sentiments and a few indiscreet comments about the missing father to farting, which apparently is no big deal in their family, either. With simple instructions and Suz's vast experience, everyone dove into their raw meat and shrimp. There wasn't a squeamish kid among us.

We each had two fondue forks the same color; in addition, we used wooden skewers I had left over from shish kebabs. The fondue forks and pot are essentially all you need to complete this dinner; they can be purchased at any kitchen store and even some in department stores. There are different fondue pots. I prefer the electric one. If you do not have the forks, you can purchase the wooden skewers at the market.

Suz was absorbed in her son's delight, as was I. We are in an easy friendship; our comfort with each other comes from exposing intimate details about our lives minus the potential threat of judgment or betrayal. We are similar in many ways, yet different enough to compliment and surprise each other still. We are goofy and never tire of silliness and the challenge of making the other laugh with outrageous behaviors that both embarrass and delight our kids. When you know someone's heart, you can wear anything to the party.

A fondue dinner can last several hours. It is combined with effortless work, some skill, and congeniality. Fondue is a good exercise in patience and tolerance—something a divorce can wear away. I didn't realize this when I decided to prepare it, but watching everyone work side-by-side, be helpful and patient when the oil burned down and new oil had to be added, and be respectful of each other's spaces, I decided it would be an exercise for couples or for anyone needing counseling for divorce or related issues.

We don't honor each other's spaces in the world, let alone at the table where often there is a rush to be served and then a frenzy to eat. Our society as a whole has expanded technology in hopes of creating more time for the family unit. Instead, there is this hysterical state of hurry-up-and-wait. It's like doing the speed limit on the freeway while being passed by people annoyed at your observation of the law. What is the big hurry? Where are we going that can't wait until the time is meant for us to arrive there? I am working on restructuring my language as well as the actions I take to enjoy the journey and to be surprised by the "ah has" of life, as my coach, Deb, says.

Here is one of my new recipes for my life, *Madame Lu's Tips for Luscious Living*: Take equal parts of time for yourself; combine slowly with dollops of those you love; liberally blend in sprinkles of responsibilities, flexibility, and tolerance with shavings of acceptance and reasonable dashes of spontaneous fun. Bake with your prayers, and give thanks until you feel warmth inside. This recipe should be seasoned to your personal taste by using the main formula: Master the art of relationships with yourself and with one another.

It's not as hokey or as difficult as you might think. Try it. What have you got to lose? Accept and be tolerant, with reason, of course, and honor each other and your promises. Write out your angry thoughts before you speak them; you'll most likely not say them. Instead, find a way to say what you need to express without as much malice.

After the last morsel of food was cooked, I unplugged the fondue pot so it could cool off. Be sure to read the cleaning directions to your pot so you don't get burned or electrocuted or ruin your pot. Suz and her girls cleared away the dinner debris while my boys illuminated the cake with nonextinguishing candles. Usually, my kids fight over who gets to put out the lights, but this time, they worked it out, and we carried John's cake to his smiling place at the head of the table. He made a wish one could only guess.

We laughed at the candles relighting themselves over and over; we can be easily amused. Suz smiled from that place inside that had shown through that day years ago in front of the school while I put the candles into a bowl of water, extinguishing them so we could eat cake.

After dinner, John let me hug him a little. "Thanks, Louie," he said.

"Anytime, John; I wanted you to know we're 'fond-a-u,' " I said, smiling.

Suz gave me a teary squeeze and wordlessly, we acknowledged and validated the emotions we needn't say out loud. The whys and should haves were behind John now, and his warm, full belly would remind him how the Master Chef in all his awesomeness provides us with the recipe for every kind of sustenance we need.

LAYER 12

Prime Rib for Patsy Walters

O God, help us not to despise or oppose what we do not

understand."

William Penn

Twice a year, for a week, I go to a place in San Diego to cleanse. My daily life with my family is a process continuously unfolding. Sometimes I get lost in all the doing, and I need to go away to regroup. I've always been the kind of person who needs time alone to refresh myself and realign my priorities. I am fortunate to have chosen a husband who accepts this about me and revels in the time he and my kids have together when I am away.

I need time to undo. I get mixed reviews about this time I take for myself, and, until recently, I had a prepared statement of validation; I created physical opportunities to allow me to go. Now, I just go. It is difficult leaving, and some visits are more successful than others, but each time, I witness miracles in myself and in others

In June of 2000, while I was at Optimum Health Institute, Patti—who is also "Patsy," my mother-in-law—struggled to breathe. For more than a year, she was plagued with a horrible cough. Her doctor was as negligent in his expedition for its cause as she was. Her hesitation, I believe, was fear-based; his was an HMO.

Most of the time, I believe in an organic approach to life, since all aspects of life are connected. I think a lot of the time, when you are plagued with a physical symptom, there is an emotional one behind it.

My best example would be a personal one. I was molested as a child, so, emotionally, I repressed my feelings of shame, pain, and disgust. My periods were very bad as a young woman. As I grew older, I manifested my guilt by creating such pain that I wound up having a series of surgeries—including a pregnancy in my fallopian tube, and having that tube and ovary removed. I was fortunate that I was able to conceive two children first, but I lost the rest and felt punished because of it. I felt that if I did enough penance, I could be forgiven; I did not, however, know how to forgive myself.

At thirty-five, my body felt ancient and foreign to me. I became addicted to being a victim. My visits to OHI peeled off layers of fragility, and I found my strength; I found my self. The more I know about my body and myself, the closer I feel to God. Now, at forty-five, I feel better than I did ten years ago; and still working on it.

While I was there in June of 2000, Patti went into the hospital with pneumonia and came out with lung cancer. I went home early and began a journey with her. I wanted to get her and bring her back to OHI with me. I have witnessed countless miracles at OHI—cancer victims taking back control of their lives and sending the disease packing. This was not an option for Patti; she felt the self-help and physical requirements would be too difficult for her. In retrospect, considering the chemotherapy and all the suffering that went with the disease, I can't understand her choice. However, I respected her and promised to support the decisions she chose. I was really pissed at the cancer, though.

I read so many books about the correlation of emotional and physical manifestations that I decided to ask the cancer directly what it would need to move on. I know how bizarre this felt, so I understand how it sounds, but I needed to feel I had control in some way. I recalled a book, *Heal Your Body, Heal Your Life,* by, Louise Hay. She cured her own cancer by releasing past experiences she had been holding onto that were making this cancer grow inside her female organs. Changing her thought patterns helped Hay heal and was the reason she wrote her book.

I left OHI early on a beautiful day; the sky looked so clear and close that I felt as though I were driving on it. God is great, I thought, yet I was confused. I didn't know how I wanted to feel. When I got home, I held each of my children tighter than usual, said a prayer of thanks, and sought my husband out for comfort from the unknown. On the way upstairs, I pulled out Louise's book. It is a handbook written in columns.

The first column is Problem. I looked up Cancer. The second column is Probable Cause. It said: "Deep hurt. Longstanding resentment. Deep secret or grief eating away at the self. Carrying hatreds. What's the use?" The third column is New Thought Pattern (to be read or written as affirmations): "I lovingly forgive and release all of the past. I choose to fill my world with joy. I love and approve of myself." Then I looked up lungs. The problem encompassed several things, including coughing and pneumonia.

"Probable Cause: Depression. Grief. Fear of taking in life. Not feeling worthy of living fully. New Thought Pattern: I have the capacity to take in the fullness of life. I lovingly live life to the fullest." I read one more "problem" because the cancer had also spread into some lymph nodes.

"Probable Cause: A warning that the mind needs to be re-centered on the essentials of life. Love and Joy.

"New Thought Pattern: I am now totally centered in the love and joy of being alive. I flow with life. Peace of mind is mine."

I read these things to my husband, who said they were unfounded. Okay, I thought, he doesn't agree with this thinking. He did want her to go to OHI, though.

We went to see Patti in St. John's hospital; her frailty and distress led me to a commitment that took on a life of its own. I felt honored and overwhelmed. I wanted to see her through this journey, perhaps because I missed the journey of my father's disappearance or death, but as I became worn down with the two-to-three-hour commute and carrying the load of two households, I began harboring some resentment toward the people I thought should have wanted to do this for her or at least to help me.

I studied my judgment, concluding much of it was based on my assumptions as well as my need to feel I was doing something for pure reasons, and, certainly, they were intended to be. I also realized I had no right to judge; my function was to bear witness and apply it to my own harbored resentments and past disappointments—judgments I held against my family; and release them.

I wrote about this and prayed for those feelings to be lifted from me, and I did keep them at bay for a long time. In the end, my grief and humanness got the best of me. I admit some feelings of resentment grew in me observing Patti's suffering. I felt abandoned that her children didn't come to see her and allowed me to carry the sole responsibility of her care. She, on the other hand, blamed their behavior on herself; her incriminating evidences designed to defend her children and pass sentence on herself gave me a great deal of respect for her as a mother. She felt that her failures to teach them what she did not offer became her burden to carry—which she did.

Patsy was the name her mother identified her as. I mention this because as her illness progressed, she fell into a child-like state. Several times toward the end of her life, she called out to her mother. Her need for childish souvenirs, stuffed animals, figurines of birds, soft-pink clothing, and food from her own childhood became the comforts a child uses to console himself.

This behavior annoyed her children, because she often spoke baby talk to them long after they were babies, and I believe it became an irritation because it reminded them of her lack of responsible mothering abilities toward them as they grew up. Perhaps they grew up faster than she.

Of course, these are my own observations and opinions based on the information Patti disclosed to me confidentially; she suffered bouts of guilt and depression throughout her illness, conceding that she should have done things differently, and she feared her children held it against her. I told her she should find comfort in the relationships she did have, and that her children loved her and would miss her, that in the end, we could all look back and say "what if" and "I should have."

In my view there were only the truths: She was young, too immature and disappointed that she was not the nucleus of her husband's world. He had to change his life, working full time instead of going to UCLA, which he had planned to. His new posture as provider, husband, and father was all new to him; he wasn't ready to settle down. Her need for his complete love and adoration escapes few of us—a fantasy especially shared by young women.

Perhaps the key is learning to balance and stay focused on adding to the empty areas of your life, which takes effort and is a constant process. Becoming a parent requires a great deal of selflessness; understanding this is neither easy nor without effort. It does have many rewards when you consider the gift you've been given—the charge of another's care, growth, and safety. It grows and changes and beats like a heart.

Patti introduced me to my husband. She had a very strong feeling we should meet, and she would not be swayed from her mission. Perhaps it was the Indian blood coursing through her veins like an old, wise woman; in any case, she was correct. I marvel at the events that lead me to my husband: My mother's friend Gail told her about the job at the Brentwood Inn—an opening for a waitress. I got the job and met Patti, who courted me to meet her son. We met on her birthday, which was also my father's birthday, and she and her son lived down the street from where I lived when I had come to L.A. Small world, as they say.

I cared for Patti a great deal, and our relationship grew stronger through the years. We were friends first, which enhanced our relationship; I could be upfront with her most of the time. It seemed natural that we should embark on this last journey together, completing it as we had begun—friends. It was far easier for me to tolerate and accept Patti, faults and neediness included; I had much less an emotional attachment then her children, which they shared as siblings.

The day I brought Patti home from the hospital, my intention was to accompany her because we had an unspoken understanding and love for each other. I wanted to enrich her remaining time here, and to make her feel loved and needed, hopefully lightening her burdens and fears in the process. I know now I had my own agenda as well—a closure to the death, which I felt robbed of when my father was gone.

It was a tedious task that I began in her home, which was dark, depressing, and oppressed from years of neglect and clutter. In an effort to hold on to the past when she was happy, she saved everything as a reminder of her youth and her babies. She still lived in the one-bedroom apartment my husband grew up in. She felt overwhelmed and embarrassed by it and refused to have visitors. I made it my quest to relieve her of that discouragement and dedicated myself to making her home the lovely, warm haven she harbored in her heart.

Though I had never before experienced this type of situation, I had an innate knowledge of what to do, and everyone came to depend on me for guidance, direction, and, in some cases, answers. It took me months of endless hours to rearrange and relieve the clutter that blocked her natural flow and to learn more about this delicate, child-like woman who would become such a part of my heart and life as never before. I would drive to her apartment from my own home in South County, at the mercy of the freeway. I listened to books on tape and made my own, releasing my feelings to the small recorder I kept with me. When Patti was lucid, I asked her questions and wrote in a journal to read later. I am still processing the words we both spoke and wrote during those eleven months.

I had no idea what I was getting into. I became a nurse, psychologist, clutter-buster, cleaning person, medical information liaison, director of two households, and student of the unknown. As Patti's illness progressed, she felt the need to be a little girl; she wanted to wear pink and behave petulantly—to be pampered the way her mother had done with her.

Though catering to these needs and deeply rooted fears went against the opinion of some, I did my best to please her. Sometimes I took on more than I should, trying to balance my family's needs with hers and neglecting myself; knowing it was temporary made the over-extension of myself easier. I grappled with the time taken away from my husband and children; they were ten and fourteen. If there was no one to keep an eye on them, they came with me, or at least one of them did; the other played at a friend's house. I would leave Sunday evenings so I could take Patti to her doctor's appointment on Monday, then spend the night so we could go to the market and stock her up on food, and then go home on Tuesday when I saw she was okay to be alone. Sometimes we would all go, taking two cars so I could stay; my husband did things around the apartment for his mother, and we would all eat together. His sister joined us or me for dinner on Sundays or Mondays, which made Patti very happy.

She wanted us to be close and stay together, especially her children, naturally. I worried about my boys having a fun summer; but when Patti saw them, she lit up. They were not always thrilled to be away from their friends, but when they saw how happy she was seeing them, they brightened up, too. We all made sacrifices for Patti; it seemed a small part for us who were healthy and strong.

My goal was to create order out of chaos, to bring light where there was darkness, and to devise a holiday for Patti that would welcome her family to her home for the last time. Patti was becoming more and more depressed as she gave into her illness and the actuality of her fate. Seeing her fall made me want to produce a joyous affair. This opportunity came with tribulations; everyone needed to conjure a festive spirit, which was difficult, to say the least. The thought of a celebration while her life faded—needing to celebrate her and her last Christmas—was bittersweet, as you could imagine.

We put up a small tree in her freshly cleaned living room, and my boys bought small decorations to hang on it; one was a small dog with a red scarf, which still sits under my car mirror. This occasion created a new independence and understanding between my children and me; I asked a lot of them, and they were generous in their efforts to comply. My husband and my sister-in-law expressed both frustration and an unrequited gratitude; they were paralyzed by their grief at losing their second parent to cancer. My niece and great-niece came, and my nephew called from North Carolina; he had his own issues to deal with.

To be honest, when the imminence of her death was actually upon us, it seemed to have snuck up unexpectedly. The doctor had been evasive for so long that when he dropped an actual timeline on me, I was hardly able to believe him.

Patti's chemo treatments were difficult on her and me; her appetite would dissipate for days at a time, leaving her weak and listless. Her depression grew mightily, overwhelming the many drugs she used to overcome these feelings. Although she had no appetite most of the time, Patti watched endless hours of cooking shows. During one of her chemo session, all of the patients in the room with her shared her optimism for the cooking shows, especially the ones that included contests like "Iron Chef."

I was acutely aware of the constant fullness of the room and the amount of people suffering from this disease. What can you say to the oncologist's staff when they can't squeeze your friend in for an appointment because there are as many in need as she? There were days I felt that I needed antidepressants; the smells that permeated from the chemicals made me so edgy that I felt giddy at times. It was not always easy to be there the entire time. I often ran to Baskin-Robins for a frozen drink to give Patti and her nurse a treat; though, in all honesty, it was as much for me as it was for them.

Patti wanted to maintain some control of her life; she chose the menu for her last Christmas celebration and admitted to me she was afraid she wouldn't make it to Christmas.

≈

Patsy Walters' Last Christmas Dinner: Prime Rib

Three Angus prime ribs (serves 8)

4 cloves garlic

1 onion chopped finely

1 teaspoon capers or ground peppercorns (depends on taste)

Salt to taste

1 tablespoon olive oil

1 Knorrs beef soup cube

2 cups water

***TIP: Cheesecloth

Pierre Bovet taught me how to make prime rib, but I have modified his recipe. Pierre was a partner in one of the best restaurants in which I have ever had the pleasure to work and eat. It was called Club Pierre-Alain, popular in the late '70s and throughout most of the '80s on Long Island. Alain Guiguet-Doran and Pierre became partners soon after the restaurant's giant success; for that union they were perfect. The Hamptons were the places to be then. Though it is still quaint and I have many friends who live there, the people who used to be considered the locals have changed considerably. On a recent visit, I realized the beaches and the beauty of the area have retained for me a whimsical paradise embedded in my memories. The years I lived there fill a chamber of my heart; for that I have endless gratitude.

I studied Pierre. His thick, French accent, deep and sexy, matched his elegant style and distinguished looks. He worked tirelessly in his kitchen dressed in designer clothes, using only a white apron folded flatteringly around his middle. He rarely soiled his garments, though he often served more than 300 meals. Pierre, who was gay, died this past year of AIDS, and I will miss him always. I gained some knowledge from every restaurant I worked in throughout my career in the business—tips, short cuts, and finesse with people—but Pierre and Alain revised my knowledge of elegance, presentation, and service.

These small, elegant, foreign men intrigued me; I felt as though I wanted to absorb their knowledge while befriending them. Each had an individual style, enchanting the young, romantic woman in me.

I didn't understand what "gay" meant, but it was so "stylish" in the '80s to be exposed to the "gay culture" surrounding the people circulating through the restaurant. The colorful characters who waltzed in and out of the elegant doors of Club Pierre certainly opened the eyes of us local bumpkins. A constant flow of homosexual men and woman as well as heterosexual people brought fame to our restaurant.

Although Pierre fascinated me, he was an enigma to me. He was obviously gay, yet he was flirtatious and debonair with women. He took me dancing one night at the Club Marakesh; we were like a pair of magic shoes fitting together perfectly.

We began a flirtation—my first with an older man; people assumed what they would; we just giggled. During our time together, he taught me many things: felicity, grace, love, and a load of great tips for the kitchen. Pierre really knew how to have a picnic - it was just like in the movies. We remained dear friends. I last saw Pierre in July of '87 on my thirtieth birthday. He had come to the West Coast to heal from the loss of his partner, Jay, who also died of AIDS. It was a wonderful reunion. He met my husband and our baby, and we spent an evening together reminiscing and creating a new, lasting memory.

On Christmas morning, I drove to Patti's with my mother after we had opened presents. My mother was visiting from South Carolina. She had been helping with Patti to give me a little break, and they became very close. It was good for Patti to have a peer with whom to speak frankly, and we all appreciated my mother's efforts. Her help enabled me to go back to OHI for a much-needed rest and regrouping. My mother is also a generous caretaker and a good friend. She was a gift to Patti; her frankness and candor, blended with her tenderness, kept Patti from feeling lonely without her friends and from feeling sorry for how her life had turned out.

On Christmas Day, I brought the food from my home in a cooler. I had requested that the butcher cut the ribs for me, as per Patti's instructions. (She liked the end cut.) When I arrived, I turned the oven up to 500, washed and patted the ribs dry, and put them aside.

In Patti's kitchen, I lightly sautéed the oil, garlic, salt, onion, peppercorns, and basil for a few minutes until they resembled cellophane. I tucked them into a piece of cheesecloth, and I squeezed and rubbed the cloth over the meat and the bones of the ribs. When done, I opened the cloth and put the contents on top of the rib meat. I put the meat into the hot oven for 15-20 minutes. I kept the meat covered with foil during this "singeing" time to keep it from drying out.

I crept quietly into Patti's bedroom. She was feeling poorly and so saddened by it. Her dream of a great last Christmas (unless we had a miracle) would not come to fruition, because she would be close to her bed much of the day. I lied down next to her, holding her fragile body and gently caressing her short hair that now grew in white and black in spots. It was a Cruella de Ville look, and she was as fashionable as she'd always been, I told her. Her skin was as soft as a baby's, and the seeming contrast between both our hands reminded me of a lady and a workingwoman. My own hands were soft but used.

"I wanted to be with my children," she choked out of labored breathing.

"I know, I know. They're coming." I comforted her as I had my own children, a tear rolled down from the corner of my eye. I knew I was escorting her from this world. My chest and throat constricted, holding back tears.

"It's Christmas," I said, "We'll make the best of it. You look beautiful, and your children will be here like every other Christmas. Don't be brave, be honest."

I believe I meant for her to cry, talk, forgive; I felt there was a lot of unresolved stuff between the three of them, and I hoped she would take this opportunity to make peace.

She did look lovely. I'd grown accustomed to her baby skin and hair. When we grow old, we become more like babies; our skin is less elastic, but soft and pale like an infant's. I sat with her until the buzzer went off. I had given her some medication so she could rest, and I knew she was emotionally waning. I wanted to respect her privacy to perhaps contemplate all the Christmases gone by.

My husband loves pearl onions in a cream sauce. I always make something special for everyone. The baby carrots in butter and parsley were my choice. I added asparagus in olive oil and lemon and pepper, and new potatoes sautéed in the pan juices from the roast, so we would have variety if not festivity. While I peeled the tiny, red potatoes, Christmas songs by a favorite group, Chicago, kept me entertained. As the CD played, I listened and peeled, peeled and thought.

Patti's children were having a difficult time with their own issues, loving and losing a second parent to this devastating disease. I discovered deep pockets of hurt in my heart for everyone—for myself. I dared not go into that place where I, too, would have to let go of this woman who was my friend and my mother-in-law and the Me Ma to my babies.

In a way, staying busy kept me from having to be completely realistic. Lord knows I had more than enough time to think; I needed to stay active so my body would not feel as heavy as my heart. I could explore and investigate each detail as it was presented to me. My way of dealing with my fear and grief was to keep us together. I was the connection and informant because it was a volunteer position.

If you don't have a steamer, place potatoes into a large Ziplok bag with about 1 cup of water, depending on the size of the bag, and microwave on high for 4 minutes (just until they are partially cooked). Add pan drippings and a few drops of olive oil for a great flavor. I sliced the potatoes, though you can quarter them as well, and put them in a covered pan, heating on medium and stirring as I heard the simmering sound get louder. The goal for this kind of potato is to soak up the juices and get crispy outside, too. My kids like these better without the onions, but I like browning a handful of sweet onions in the drippings before I put the potatoes in. A trick I use to get my kids past the fear of onions is to slice them paper-thin and use small, sweet onions; I love Maui and Vidalia.

I checked again on Patti, who had burrowed into her leopard snuggly throw, which had become a sort of security blanket for her. Her breathing was regular, and I found my own breath escaping in a sigh as I had been holding it in without realizing. I don't think I had a security blanket as a child; my kids do, though, and they still secretly rely on the comfort it brings. I crossed through the apartment, enjoying the newly installed carpet and linoleum. These simple though tedious tasks brought so much change in the apartment and in Patti; her delight in padding around barefooted without slippers for protection brought a smile to my lips every time. I hugged myself for making all the arrangements and seeing to the details to bring this gift to a woman who had brought me my husband through her intuitive enthusiasm. I lost so much when she died, yet what I gained are living in my children and will continue with God's will in theirs for generations to come.

The potatoes called me; I stirred them and turned the heat down a little. I lowered the oven temperature to 375 and basted the ribs. Following the same directions put the carrots went into the same bag as the potatoes; add fresh water to get rid of extra starch. They cook faster than the potatoes, so I put them aside.

My husband and children arrived just after three when I woke Patti so she would feel alert in her greeting. Patti's daughter, Linda, arrived, followed by her daughter, Ami, and her granddaughter Laurie. While the cranberries, orange peels, raisins, and chutney simmered on low heat in brown sugar and orange juice, we commenced opening gifts. Linda had made her mother a turquoise beaded necklace. It was beautiful; each bead was separated by a red, knotted string. Patti was delighted, but after twenty minutes she was exhausted. Chris and Linda helped her back to bed; the three of them had a good visit, I think.

Ami and I went to the kitchen while I washed and cut the bottoms off the asparagus. It is good to be the chef because everyone comes into the kitchen eventually and usually alone. I have been chastised for hiding away in the kitchen, but it is really my devised plan of luring everyone to me. It gives us each time to speak freely and catch up on the time we have been out of touch. I feel at home in any kitchen once I am at work.

I like to take a good inch or so off of the bottom of the asparagus and remove the small leaves that can get tough when cooked. I placed them in another plastic bag with a few tablespoons of water and a sprinkle of lemon pepper, and set them aside. The roast cooked for the better part of 2½ hours. I took it out so it could cool off and steamed the carrots and asparagus. I mixed the carrots with a handful of fresh chopped parsley and ½ of one small stick of butter (per 1 pound bag).

The asparagus got light olive oil, about a teaspoon more of lemon pepper, and a small pat of butter. In the meantime, I poured just under a cup of unsweetened heavy cream and 3 tablespoons of butter into a saucepan with the pearl onions I'd prepared earlier. I sprinkled a touch of salt and pepper to taste, and Patti, following her nose into the kitchen, snuck her favored dash of nutmeg into the onions; they simmered on a low-medium heat until the sauce became thick and creamy. ***TIP when heating cream or milk, stir continually to prevent ingredients from sticking to the bottom of the pan.

We ate buffet style; I was pleased that everything came out at the same time and that I hadn't forgotten or burned anything. I was happy to see Patti prepare a small dish of horseradish sauce (sour cream and horseradish to taste), though she had a difficult time with even this small task. Our dinner ended, and I cleaned up the kitchen while Linda spoke about her illustrious love life with her then beau, Barney.

Linda was living in Amsterdam with Barney, sadly, our family has scattered. When we were all together; time fell away, closing the gap. I enjoy the closure of cleaning up the kitchen after I have cooked a big meal; it helps me digest everything, including my food. As I stood alone at the sink while Linda and Chris sat on the bed with a weepy Patti, I fought back a sob, knowing the moment would never be repeated. I had shared nineteen Christmas's with this family, which kept getting smaller. I was powerless; yet, in that same instant, I realized the power shift. We'd had this many; they were all great, and our time felt precious. I had shared fewer Christmas's with my father; I felt the bittersweet comfort of something lost, something gained.

Grateful that I could conduct a meal and orchestrate this reunion, I felt tired and overwhelmed with the knowledge that this would be the last time I would cook for us all together. I was saddened further by the absence of my nephew, Eric, Linda's son who lived in North Carolina, but such is life. Finally, I breathed deeply, touched up my melted face, and went into the bedroom to witness the communion of mother and children.

Patti had confessed to me that her shortcomings as a mother had alienated her children from her to a degree. I knew the way my husband felt, as much as he'd confided through silence and words, and Linda had confessed her feelings where her mother was concerned many times. I saw three people aching to touch their feet on the same ground being comforted by the togetherness they had created in the dance of life they did together. It is erroneous to compare your particular dance with any other you share a relationship with; each step is as individual as the foot it steps in the company of.

When we left, I held Patti to me while her tears welled up again. She thanked me and apologized for being sick.

"Hey," I said, "cancer sucks, and you having it sucks even more, but never apologize to me because you are and will always be my dear, sweet friend."

"I love you," she said, and settled into her bed for a long-awaited rest.

"Sweet dreams," I said. "Sweet dreams."

LAYER 13

Brownie Mush with Valentine Stew

"Love is an action, an activity. It is not a feeling."

M. Scott Peck

Donna Reed was my hero. I watched her lovely and well dressed on television, wearing pearls as she effortlessly maintained her home, fed her kids "healthy," well-balanced meals, kept her husband happy, smiled, and played cards with the girls. All this, and still she had time to volunteer with various charities. Her dinner table was a source of lively conversation combined with parental direction and love. Donna created the facade of a perfect life—a perfect woman.

The Donna Reed show was wildly popular because it massaged people's internal fears and provided them with guidelines so they were able to model their own family's welfare with the same grace as Donna; before women's lib shook the axiom, eroding the role of each sex. As I grew up, television mothers changed. Donna Reed gave way to Florence Henderson, who slid over for Mrs. Partridge, who went into the country to meet Mrs. Walton, and Mrs. Ingles eventually morphing into Roseanne, a woman with whom I could relate to my own childhood.

I began seeing my "mother role" as that of an artist—a woman with many "hats," so to speak. As times changed and the Information Age began to desensitize us of our comforts, I learned to research, experiment, and filter, discarding and modifying my position as CEO of my household with greater confidence I embraced my new role as a "domestic engineer", my husband's endearing title for me; with enthusiasm.

I learned that though I eat a mainly vegetarian diet, my kids would not be robbed of their childhood by being denied Kool-Aid, chocolate, s'mores, and all manor of junk foods. I began to see that a clean house did not necessarily mean a happy one, or that "order" meant working well. I took charge of my decisions, guarded my secrets, and validated my choices by not allowing anyone to barge into my comfort zone. This has taken some time, and I have learned many lessons from my children—sometimes more than once. Often, I do not catch on right away and need time to process and make mistakes, which they graciously allow me. That said, I give you a meal filled with sugar, salt, red meat, preservatives, some healthy ingredients, and as much fun as I can muster up for my kids' Valentine's Day.

I should give you a little background about Valentine's Day and me. For twenty-three years, Valentine's Day has been the anniversary of my father's disappearance. (He was in the Mafia and was arrested and disappeared. He is thought by many to be dead; the jury is still out with me.) In the beginning, I had a difficult time with the anniversary, especially when I was single and had no one to comfort me with love. After I met and married my husband, I had the perks, but that null and void feeling stayed with me for a long time, like a bad hangover from cheap wine—an experience not worth repeating.

Tiring of this absurd sense of loyalty to feel "down" on that day, I decided it was time to alter the tradition. My father loved a party and a good meal, so in honor of him and us, new memories were created hosting a Valentine's parties with a themes.

The first was a red pajama party, which was great! Everyone participated by wearing some kind of red PJs, and it was a blast. The second party was the 20th anniversary of my dad's disappearance; so I transformed our backyard into THE GROTTO OF THE PURPLE GRAPE. The Grotto was one of the 52 establishments that my father, a true entrepreneur was the architect of. He was ahead of his time; so far he never caught up with himself; and no one else caught up with him—until now. The dress was a mafia theme; everyone was very creative. I always have some kind of entertainment: for the mafia party, we had the "Trivia Godfather," the Italian opera-singing magician, and, naturally, "Frank Sinatra"—well, his comedic, singing, wanna-be (but not at all a look-alike!). For a recent party, everyone had to bring a joke and wear red. I hired a comedian, but the guests' jokes were priceless. Each year people, begin calling in January to make sure they have the date cleared on their calendars. It has been a successful way to overcome a devastating loss. We toast his life and accept his disappearance, yet it is still a reminder that I will most likely never know what happened to him.

I usually reserve the actual Valentine's Day for my kids. This past year, I chose Mush Brownies because they are sinfully gooey and yummy and beef stew because my kids will eat it and enjoy it, veggies and all. My beef stew is a variation of my mother's and other strangers I have encountered, but mostly, it is designed to appeal to my family's tastes.

This year, I shopped with a wet head of freshly permed hair. My market is Pavilion's because there is no Gelson's or Gristede's. It is my day to carpool for junior high, so with my groceries in tow, I rush to pick up. It is 3:11 p.m. when we get home, and my youngest son has gymnastics at 3:30 p.m., so I put away the perishables and drive to the gym. He shares his day and his many Valentines with me; he's gotten thirty-one! At gymnastics, he is beginning a new level with a new instructor, so, although he will act like I'm not really necessary, he wants me to walk him in. I cherish these times I am still needed by my boys; they become so adult and independent so fast.

While he's practicing, I go to the local stores to put together some gifts for them—a cool bath-salt ball with a coupon good for one massage and one "mommy-made" bath, a coupon for Starbucks, a cylinder of mini-M&Ms, and a bookmark with a manly heart on it.

I like to mail my kids their cards and write them letters; I believe in celebrating and creating rituals. I have begun and passed on rituals for holidays, as well as everyday events. My kids love these small tokens—heirlooms to cherish and share. Boys need this type of promise—this keepsake and this continuity—as much as any girl I've ever met, and often more. They share them with their friends, and the custom or ritual expands beyond my wildest imagination. Our world is vast; having small ways of feeling connected to it are essential acts of joy. Is there a more fulfilling feeling than joy from love? I think not.

At home, I start the stew. My son dances into the kitchen a sort of karate-waltz, his personal style, excited and delighted to have a celebration with all of us together—with presents! Humans need rituals! We need celebrations of life from start to finish, benchmarks of our time spent on top and in the trenches of daily living. What could be more important than gauging our experiences with glorifications and benedictions than celebrating our daily living?

We don't need a holiday to create a ritual; anytime a shift is needed, create a celebratory ritual. Here is one to look forward to any day, compliments of Wendy Nichols, my friend from the seventh grade: When you see a moving mail truck, cross your fingers and make a wish or say a prayer. You must see a dog to uncross your fingers and get your wish. I cannot stop myself from this silly act, and happily, it gives us a million times a day to think of something else—a promise or a wish. It's a feel-good thing, simple fun like making a wish on the first star or when you see a rainbow. I have shared these ceremonies with so many adults now, and they do them, too. You'd be amazed how such a small shift can brighten your mood. We all need to tap into that part of us that is childish in a good way.

≈

Brownie Mush with Valentine Stew

1 pound stew meat (I use sirloin; there is usually precubed meat available.

***TIP: if you use a lower grade of meat, cook longer on lower heat.

3 celery stalks

4 carrots

4 red potatoes

1 onion (any color)

2 tablespoons beef soup base (I use Better-Than-Bouillon, which comes in a jar, or MBJ packets)

2 tablespoons olive oil

1 teaspoon lemon pepper

1 teaspoon crushed garlic

Let stew simmer until the meat is tender (2-3 hours); add the quick-cooking vegetables about 15 minutes before serving so they are not mushy. Start the brownies when you sit down to eat so you can ice them hot. They taste best when eaten with a spoon.

Before I cook, I chose a movie; it relaxes me while I cook. I often view a movie I've seen before so I am free to roam from room to room and chore to chore without the worries of missing a part or being overly drawn in. This time, I chose *French Kiss*. I have watched it many times; it's hysterical!

Use a large quart pan to start; pour 2-3 tablespoons of olive oil to coat the bottom. Chop onions and celery, adding seasonings, and let them sauté. Wash and pat dry the beef, cutting pieces the size you prefer; my kids don't like them too big or too chewy, so I cut them smaller. Put them into a large Ziploc bag or paper bag with flour and salt. Coat meat, then add to onions and celery for browning. The flour on the meat serves as a thickening agent for the stew. Peel potatoes and carrots; cut them to the size you prefer. The size makes a difference to some; my husband won't eat a carrot that is too big or too small. Partially presteam potatoes. I use a Ziploc here again: put 2-3 tablespoons of water in and seal it. Put in microwave for about 4 minutes. I will say here and now I know "nuking" the veggies kills most of the nutrients, but my kids like them semi-soft and if I don't have a lot of time, that's what I do. I chose my own theory of moderation.

While I am waiting for the veggies to steam in the microwave, I focus on the movie. Kevin Klein has just stolen a car; while the alarm is screaming, Meg Ryan asks him his name. In his special French accent he says, "Bob." Ryan repeats what she hears, "Bub," and he corrects her until she gets it right. It's the "Oui, Bob" scene and so funny. I don't know why this tickles me so, but I have often used this line in conversation to see if anyone will bite.

Once, on vacation in St. Barths, I tried that line to feed my appetite for comedy. To my delight, it was not lost on the recipient. My friend Kim and I were "maids" in Rosemary's wedding here on this island, a lush tropical paradise. My angelic husband manned the home front and our children so I could come. (I am so blessed.) We were stretching and splashing around our pool at the Village St. Jean, a beautiful, quaint set of cottages nestled a few minutes up the hill from the town of St. Jean.

We were terribly giddy spending this luscious time together (we now live on opposite coasts), laughing in our pool, when we were interrupted by another hotel guest. I was exercising in the pool, and the gentleman commented that vacations were not for exercising. We bantered easily among the three of us, and he introduced himself as Bob. I suppose it was the good mood and the "French" thing; anyway, for some reason, I repeated his name using Kevin Klein's heavy accent, whereupon he answered, "Oui, Bob." I shrieked at his witty comeback and reveled in his understanding.

Okay, rent the movie and you will perhaps be able to share in the joke or not. I love to laugh, don't you?

Before I added the veggies I boiled 2-3 cups of water, depending on how many I am serving. When the water boiled, I poured it into the pot and added the soup base (or bouillon), stirring until there was no sign of paste. I covered it and let it simmer on very low heat. I had to pick up my son, so I turned the heat off, which is okay for a short time.

***TIP: If you stop cooking meat that needs to cook a long time to become tender, and cook it again later on low, it prepares nicely.

I got caught in a voracious downpour. After five minutes of solid rain (literally—it hailed), the sun emerged, and I was privy to my second rainbow in a week! Emerging from the gym, my son smiled just for me, and we walked hand-in hand. We chased down the remains of the rainbow, made our wish, and went home.

At home, we resumed our duties—mine, cooking and setting the places at the table with specialized Valentine's goodies; his, joining the game already in progress in the street of our cul-de-sac. I am acutely aware of these everyday moments of our life. I try to observe what is often taken for granted, and I am always rewarded for my efforts.

Meg Ryan made me wish I had short hair, while I sliced the bread and my stew bubbled its ingredients into perfect edibility. We brought our bounty to the table, exchanged gifts (mine was a wonderful set of hanging Cloister Bells; I love chimes), then gave thanks, toasted my dad wherever he may be, and enjoyed our stew. Joy should always be this effortless.

Before I sat down, Betty Crocker's fudge brownie mix (smart size) went into the oven. The oven's timer went off during dinner. I cooked the brownies approximately five minutes less than the recommended time so they would be mushy.

While my boys cleared the table, I iced the brownies. This time, I used chocolate and vanilla, because they were left over. The icing melts into the gooey brownies immediately. Add a scoop of French Vanilla ice cream into each bowl, and then spoon a portion of the brownies onto it. Yummy!

By now, the day is coming to an end. My heart skips a beat, thinking that another year has come and gone with still no idea of my father's whereabouts. Is he dead, chopped into tiny pieces for fish chum somewhere over the Everglades? This is what my brother and mother believe. Or is he living the life he dreamt of, tucked neatly into some small, indiscreet beach town with a new identity and family? I don't allow myself to linger on these questions for very long because I indulged in that crazy scenario for too long, and, as I said, that is another recipe book entirely. As time goes on,

I find it is not so much the man I miss anymore, but the presence of a father, which I suppose I will always long for.

I hope you enjoy your rendition of the Valentine's meal; enjoy your family, friends, life. After all, who's to say what tomorrow will bring?

LAYER 14

Meatballs, Pasta & Peace

"And forgive us our trespasses, as we forgive those who trespass against us."

Matthew 6:12

I thought I was finished, but while editing this book; our world has experienced unthinkable terrorist attacks and maintained substantial emotional damage and devastation. Witnessing these incredulous events is beyond surreal, beyond Hollywood. I sat glued to the television, listening to our President say words like "bellicose" and "pugnacious," and though I certainly got the context, I looked them up, furthering my sense of outrage. I carry my feelings as though I would barter them for a new set, while newly acquainted strangers bombard me with their silent torpor.

I do not want more bloodshed. I do not want vengeance. I do not wish to be idle. I wish we could find a way to give them back their oil and rid those oppressed countries from the fear and hatred of terrorists by sticking those murdering fanatics in a spaceship and launching it to some unknown, uninhabited planet with no women to procreate with and then restore peace to the world.

On the other hand, I want this opportunity to be the vehicle for change, to enlighten, to act from a place of peace and love, not fear and intolerance. I am Pollyanna in my wishes, a battle maid in my thoughts and an American in my actions; I am appalled that people who cry peace scream their hatred of the President. On the other hand, I am exhilarated at the activity our country participates in, the apathy falling aside for a time.

Sometimes I tire from putting such effort into someone else's needs as I often do, yet continuing to do so keeps me humbled to my own needs—not to ignore them, but not to let them take control of me. During a memorial service at our parish, the priest said something that resonates in my heart and mind; it is a core belief of mine: "Hate the sin, not the sinner." His words gave me peace; they gave me a vehicle for my prayers, which were selfish and vast. I prayed after that to heal the hearts of those who have fallen; to lighten the darkest of hearts obscured by the evil stoking soul-less deeds of the wicked. I am not naive, though I disliked believing in pure evil; I have seen, with my own eyes, the boogeyman is real.

In praying like this, I feel impartial, as though my prayer is a blanket that covers multitudes, segregating no one. Since I needed to reach out, to move out of my small life yet still be connected to it, I felt the necessity to reclaim what the terrorists tried to rob; not only our sense of safety, but our belief in human kind. This last layer was then added; and one more recipe.

The shrimp and vegetable dish is for me, while the spaghetti and meatballs are for my kids. I served them under the umbrella— my recipe for peace of mind after a week of horror and fear; only the beginning I feared.

I needed to do something to contribute to the mending of our world. I had this lyric playing in my mind over and over, "Let there be peace on earth, and let it begin with me." I was nervous, but I figured it would be safe to reach out to my immediate community, our neighborhood.

I put my flag on my car and flew another in front of my home. I went to church several times to light candles and lay my intentions in the hands of God, and I sent a letter to my neighbors asking them to meet us on Sunday evening with a candle and a prayer for unity and to share stories of our feelings and experiences of the week's nightmare. I had no idea what it would be like, but I had a prayer I wrote, and I wanted to share it.

I invited my mother and her roommate for dinner before the vigil. My husband said he did not want her roommate to come to our home. So, a healing needed to take place there, too. I believe he was uncomfortable with the fact that the roommate was once a lover of his deceased mother. Since my mother and Patti, my mother-in-law, lived together in a condo we all purchased for a short while before Patti died, much of her furniture was still in the condo, including her bed. It had only been five months since her death. For me, the full circle of her ex, now my mother's roommate, resting in the very bed in which he slept with Patti, was a comfort, and I felt she would be smiling from heaven as well. I can understand how her son felt this was strange, but I'm a die-hard sometimes, and I felt he should know that this man had truly cared for his mother in his own way.

Sunday, September 15, 2001, the end of a week that scorned our freedom. In an effort to feel better, I shopped for food; everything else felt small.

While cruising through the busy market, the large shrimp caught my eye in the seafood counter. I never tire of shrimp, though some critics of the health community are saying some ugly things about them. I'm sick of the news; one week, seafood is good for you and red meat is not, and the next, it's reversed. If we listen to everything "they" say, we'll enjoy nothing; it's getting crazy. I figure I'll die of something, hopefully later than sooner, so I bought two pounds of shrimp. As I moved along the aisles, a familiar smell caught my nose's attention, and then it was gone. I walked the store looking for it, realizing when I stood next to the butcher's counter; it was a perfume that Patti had worn.

My boys like spaghetti and my meatballs. They eat other meatballs, but always tell me mine are better. Isn't that sweet? I bought ground sirloin, tomatoes, angel-hair pasta (which is all they will eat with sauce), and salad stuff, including hearts of palm, black olives, and sprouts. My salads are serious meals.

When I got home, I put on the television. A journalist was speaking with a group of children from New York City about post-9/11 feelings. It was refreshing and prodigious hearing our youth speak their hearts and minds. Our children are our future; it's a cliché, but it is the absolute truth. It makes me angry that marvelous kids go unnoticed when the media can latch onto a tragic story pigeon holing kids in negative light. I was touched with their sentiments; I wiped tears from my eyes while making meatballs.

My recipe varies because I add grilled onions, parsley, and oregano when I'm making them for adults. My kids don't like to see the "green stuff" and onions. So while honoring their developing taste buds, I give you the recipe for the kids' meatballs:

≈

Meatballs

2 pounds ground beef (I prefer sirloin.)

1 egg

1 tablespoon oyster sauce

1 tablespoon soy sauce

4 tablespoons breadcrumbs (I use Progresso.)

Lemon pepper to taste (approximately 1 teaspoon.)

Garlic salt to taste (approximately 1 teaspoon.)

1 teaspoon freshly grated Parmesan cheese

Combine all ingredients in any order; knead together.

***TIP: I wear rubber gloves to mush these ingredients because it spares my hands and blends everything well.

Roll ground beef into balls. Bake at 400 in a glass Pyrex dish for 20 minutes or until the meat is browned well and the texture is firm—not hard though, or it will be dry. Normally, I would have prepared tomato sauce prior to making the meatballs, but I had some homemade sauce frozen from the week before. I will give you that recipe, too.

While I ran water into a large pasta pot, my attention came back to the television; a young woman expressed a distressing emotion. She was keenly aware of the ramifications posing such a point of view, and I was proud of her for her bravado.

She asked, "Don't you think the people of Pakistan and Afghanistan are thinking we are getting a taste of our own medicine?"

The host took a noticeable deep breath and replied by asking if anyone would like to respond—quite the diplomatic evasion on his part.

A composed, self-assured young man with shaggy, black hair raised the microphone to his lips and spoke in a firm but kind voice. He said we may have bombed other countries, but we had a reason; we didn't just attack innocent people. The young woman's response was heightened by her body language, shifting her posture to appear taller and facing the young man directly. Her response was indignant as she expressed her disagreement, saying that we certainly have killed innocent people. The young man adjusted his body, intending, it seemed, to defend his statement and our country's previous actions, when the host stepped in and said, "This is a large and difficult subject, and we honor your opinions, but we need to move on."

These fine lines of life carry us over the fence and at other times under it, sliding narrowly through the well-worn hole of others before us.

I wondered just how we would move on. How do you move on from something unimaginable? I was so engrossed in the debate of these young people that I had chopped Maui onions, bok choy, celery, parsley, garlic, zucchini, and water chestnuts into a large frying pan with olive oil without realizing it. So, I went with it, adding dried dill, fresh basil, thyme, soy sauce, ground pepper, and a rosemary mint that began growing wildly in my back yard. I let these ingredients sauté while I cleaned and deveined the shrimp. Here are the ingredients for the second first course:

≈

2 Maui onions (small-medium sized)

2 large stalks bok choy

3 stalks celery

Fresh parsley

1 zucchini

1 can water chestnuts

1 tablespoon dill

1 tablespoon basil

1 tablespoon thyme

1 pinch rosemary mint

2 cloves garlic

1 pound fresh, raw shrimp

Drain shrimp and pat them dry, then about 10 minutes before serving, lower heat and add to sautéed mixture. While everything is cooking, prepare the salad. I am a big salad person and have become daring with unconventional additions to enhance a basic salad.

My Nani makes my favorite salad, though. She uses iceberg lettuce, black olives, a little olive oil and lemon, and a dash of salt.

Perhaps it is because she makes it. I'm not sure; I just know I love it.

Salads are often a meal for me; sometimes I eat two a day, so I enjoy experimenting. This time, I crumbled sunflower and sesame crusts, pieces of dried cranberry, and leftover pickled snap peas.

Salad dressing

½ cup olive oil, light and virgin (*** TIP: Olive oils have distinctive tastes. For a salad, I use the lightest one I can find unless it's for a Caesar.)

Equal parts of balsamic vinegar and rice vinegar to taste (About 3 tablespoons altogether.)

Splash of Memmi sauce (This is actually a Japanese soup base sauce that looks like soy sauce.)

Garlic salt to taste (Or if you crush fresh garlic, use straight salt.)

Dash fresh ground pepper medley

Grated cheese on top (I use fontina, Parmesan, or provolone— or all 3.)

Homemade Tomato Sauce with Melinda's Tomatoes

Tomato sauce from fresh tomatoes:

1-2 dozen homegrown tomatoes (My neighbor, Melinda, has a green thumb; her tomatoes are as sweet as any summer fruit, so we have a deal. She gives me the tomatoes and I make the sauce, which we split. It's a nice arrangement.)

1 medium-sized sweet onion, finely chopped

2 stalks celery

4 leaves fresh mint, finely chopped*

3 leaves fresh basil, finely chopped*

3-5 leaves fresh oregano, finely chopped*

2 cloves garlic, minced

Salt and pepper to taste

1-2 tablespoons balsamic vinegar or red wine

* Dried herbs can be substituted.

My boys set the table on the patio to enjoy the lovely weather. My kids are excited about the candlelight vigil—all of their friends are coming. They wanted to have the opportunity to do something in the face of this horror. I teach my kids how to create order out of chaos; it got me through tough times as a kid and still does. We all need to feel in control of something these days. Sadly, children are often dismissed during a crisis or tragedy instead of being given opportunities to do something that gives them a sense of power. Parents put their fears on their kids inadvertently, and kids need a way, their own way, to feel and express their feelings.

I could hear my boys discussing the folding of napkins and placement of forks; they took over the table setting. I am thrilled when my kids work together willingly; it gives me great pleasure.

They spoke of who would be coming to the vigil, how some people had cousins or friends who were lost in the fire rescues. I felt a pride in their understanding of a tragedy of such magnitude. My kids were fourteen and ten when this happened, and, though I expose them to many real issues, I am always amazed at what they choose to take an interest in; this was definitely one of those times.

While we were getting ready for our guests, my husband was printing a peace prayer from our church to hand out at the vigil. We all needed to do something. It was our way of contributing. People need to be in relationships with each other, with nature, even machines connect and stregnthen our tolerance to what is foreign to us. Relationships create a vehicle for acceptance, community-knowledge, and growth. It is through each relationship that our progression in life enhances our consciousness. In these dances, we are forced to see that there are vulnerabilities to be respected and acknowledged ours and others'. Relationships are designed to keep us on our toes, sometimes challenged. They are proposals: "Can we master and homor? Can we nod our heads in agreement to disagree? Can we embrace our own imperfections mirrored in another?"

So, there we were doing something in the face of this fear, the unknown, progressing on in our own ways. I was removing the meatballs; Chris was printing the prayer, and my boys were setting the table for our meal. Even my mother called to say they were stopping for wine and that she was bringing extra candles. They, too, were immersed in their own pursuit of taking action.

The host wrapped up his show. I blotted the meatballs on a paper towel and carefully put them into the simmering tomato sauce. I use long tongs for this job so I won't get burned if the meatballs splash into the sauce. Once submerged, I stirred them, making sure the sauce was not sticking to the bottom of the pan. I switched off the television and turned on the stereo; music soothes me. I turned off the oven and placed the loaf of bread into it to keep it warm. I drained the pasta. put it into a large bowl sprinkled salt and olive oil on it while I gently manipulated the noodles so they would not stick. Then I put a cover on it and placed it back on the still-hot burner, though no heat was turned on. I was pretty much ready to serve. When my mother arrived, I put the shrimp into the pan and prepared each dish for the table. I tossed the salad, and when all was on the table, we said a blessing and ate.

We discussed the terrorist attacks, sharing our information in a noncombative conversation—each with their own views, though careful not to impose them on anyone else. We were a diverse group. Tonight we chose to tread lightly.

At 6:05, I excused myself to write out my prayer and prepare for the vigil. The sun was beginning to rest, and as I opened the front door, I could see several of my neighbors walking toward the park, children with candles in hands. I felt a gratifying sense of pride. I was nervous because I had the feeling people expected me to know what I was doing, so I did what I always do in these situations. I act like I have done this a thousand times, pray for guidance, though I admitted to my virginity. The group was pretty large.

We illuminated our candles and, fortunately, I had several extras. I was anxious, so I got right to welcoming and thanking everyone for their support. I read my prayer way too fast because I became choked up, and when I finished, I stepped out of the circle. There were expectant looks on everyone's faces, so I asked if anyone would like to speak, share, or lead us in a prayer. My husband did. He claims he is not comfortable speaking in public, but he did an excellent job—much better than me. I was touched and proud. Several more people emerged from the hill, and we enlarged our circle to include everyone. By this time, we had a large group. Again, I asked if anyone wished to speak, and each time, someone did.

My oldest son came and whispered in my ear, "Mom shouldn't we pray for President Bush to be guided to make the right decisions?" I am so proud of my kids. A firefighter led us in a prayer asking for our blessings for those selfless heroes, which brought many of us to tears. In a cracked, emotional voice, another neighbor shared that his son's close friend had three cousins in New York—all firefighters, and all missing. My previous neighbor shared her experience as a flight attendant stranded in Oakland for three days, surrounded by women with husbands missing in the World Trade Center. It was tendor and raw and empowering; and so very real.

After we had prayed and shared, I asked that we blow out our candles together and make a wish for our country. Then, I gathered all the children to hold a part of the bunch of balloons and release them together. We hugged and said goodbye; people thanked me for bringing us together. I was content to feel united, with mutual intentions and shared affection; it made me proud to be an American. The culmination of each action and each intention I exuded that day added to the already powerful force that is humanity. We digested each other's sorrow, fears, hopes, and gladness, needing individually and collectively to be sustained by one another.

I will leave you with the prayer I wrote; I hope you will take it if it serves you and release it if it does not. But more importantly, I hope it blesses you.

Dear God,

Help us stay in this heightened state of spiritual awareness. Let us not be absorbed by the roller coaster of humanity, which may sweep us from the strength of our faith as it is now, in this dire time and stay with us always, especially when we are safe and comfortable and not in need. Thank you, Amen.

ACKNOWLEDGEMENTS

This could be a book in itself: Thank you, Pat Craig, for telling me I was beyond college writing, to move forward, Thank you Debra Valle for guiding, gluing, and greatly supporting my efforts to start and finish this book; Rosemary, for reading the first draft and telling me she was inspired to write her own book, always asking and loving me through; Kim, for my graphics and on each page and her "Chicky" is displayed. Everyone from the "title party"—you are all going to be mentioned on my Web site; Victoria Giraud for her editing help, Carrie for her much needed organization efforts; Pat Rogers for his amazing photographic gifts, and making me look good on the covers; Patrick is too humble about his gifts. LoriAnne for her friendship, and efforts in helping to move me forward; Traci for her friendship, support help with my Web site, as well as Derek for saying my book moved him; and everyone I know for asking, supporting, and encouraging me, including Gerry, my bestest-long time friend for wanting to have been here; though she is aways, in my heart. For Suzy for reading and praising; and Ron, who has always wanted me to be the Mafia daughter I am.

But my life would be colorless without my family—my husband, who without a hand book loves and supports me still; my sons, Sean, who came up with the title, and Evan, for hugs, kisses, support and humor and for their love; and to my first family, Mommy and Victor:

I love you all, endlessly.

Made in the USA
Middletown, DE
15 June 2023

32655423R00156